スター・ウォーズ

新たなる希望〈上〉

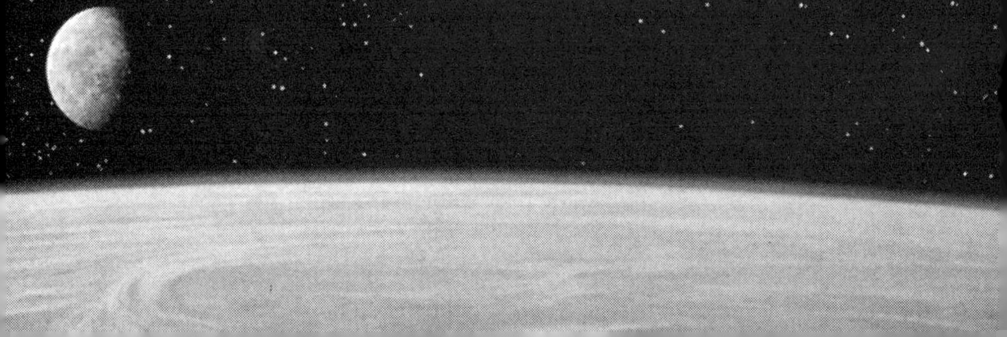

"WHERE DO YOU THINK YOU'RE GOING?"

STAR WARS: A NEW HOPE — MANGA is a translation which was first published in Japan by Media Works. In Japan, manga is normally read from right-to-left. In order to conform to Western standards, the art in this book was copied in a mirror-image to facilitate left-to-right reading of the pages. This, of course, can cause some confusion in a story such as STAR WARS: A NEW HOPE — MANGA where readers are somewhat familiar with the material and so will notice characters both moving and appearing in an opposite fashion from that which they did in the film. We apologize for any confusion this may cause and hope that it will not detract from your enjoyment of this volume.

ピ
いいか もう私を当てにするなよ 絶対に助けてやらないからな
これ以上わけのわからないことに巻き込まれるのはもうごめんだよ！

WHAT MISSION? WHAT ARE YOU TALKING ABOUT?
I'VE JUST ABOUT HAD ENOUGH OF YOU! GO THAT WAY!
YOU'LL BE MAL-FUNCTIONING WITHIN A DAY, YOU NEARSIGHTED SCRAP PILE!
VEE-BEE! BOOP!

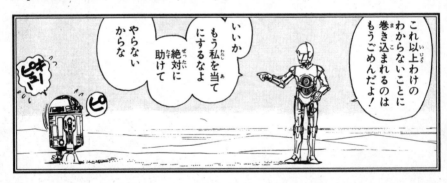

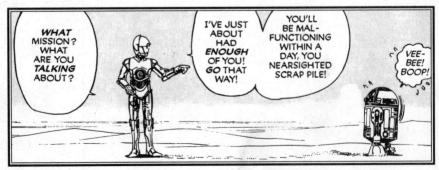

A long time ago in a galaxy far, far away....

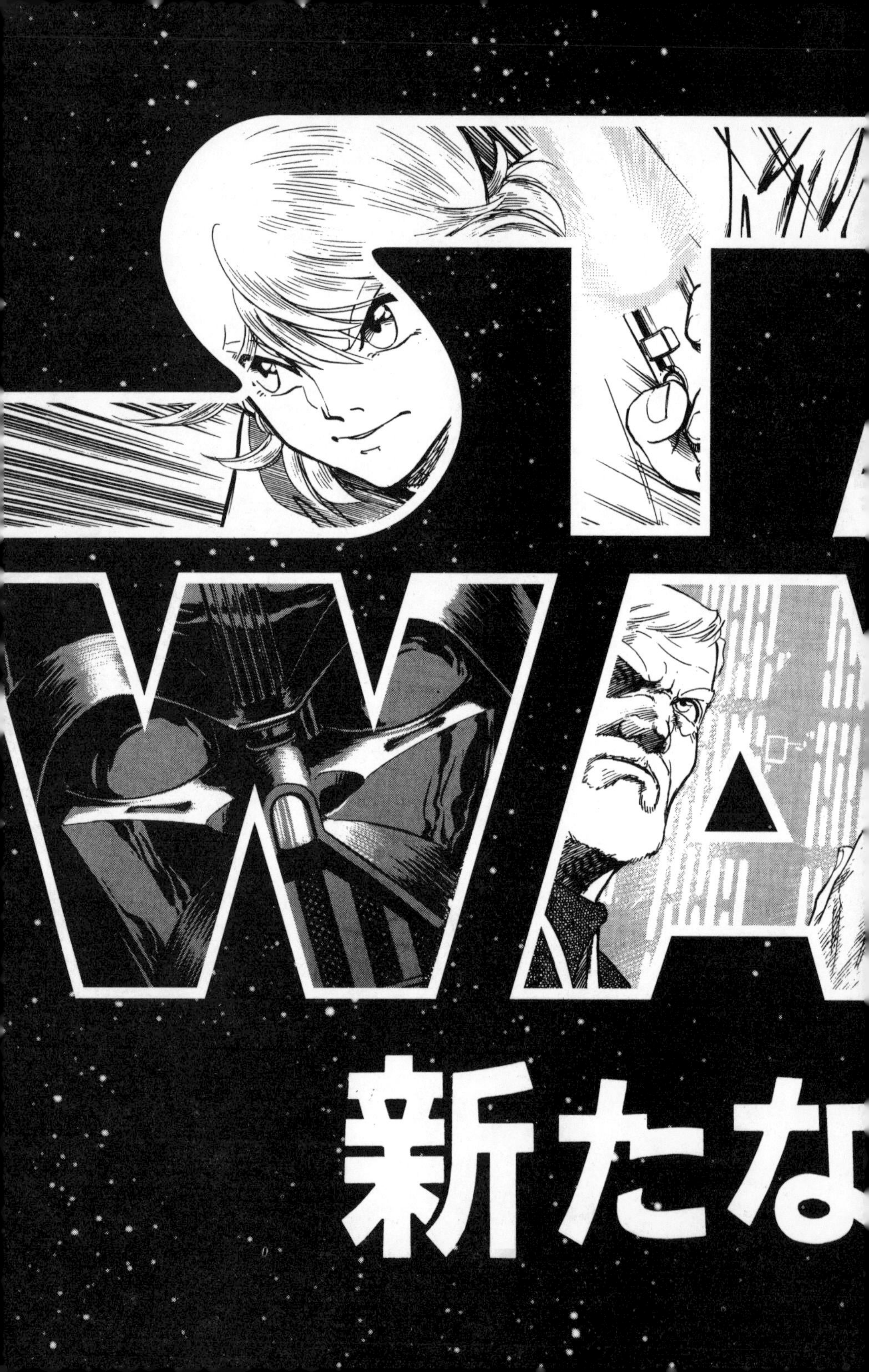
STA
WA
新たな

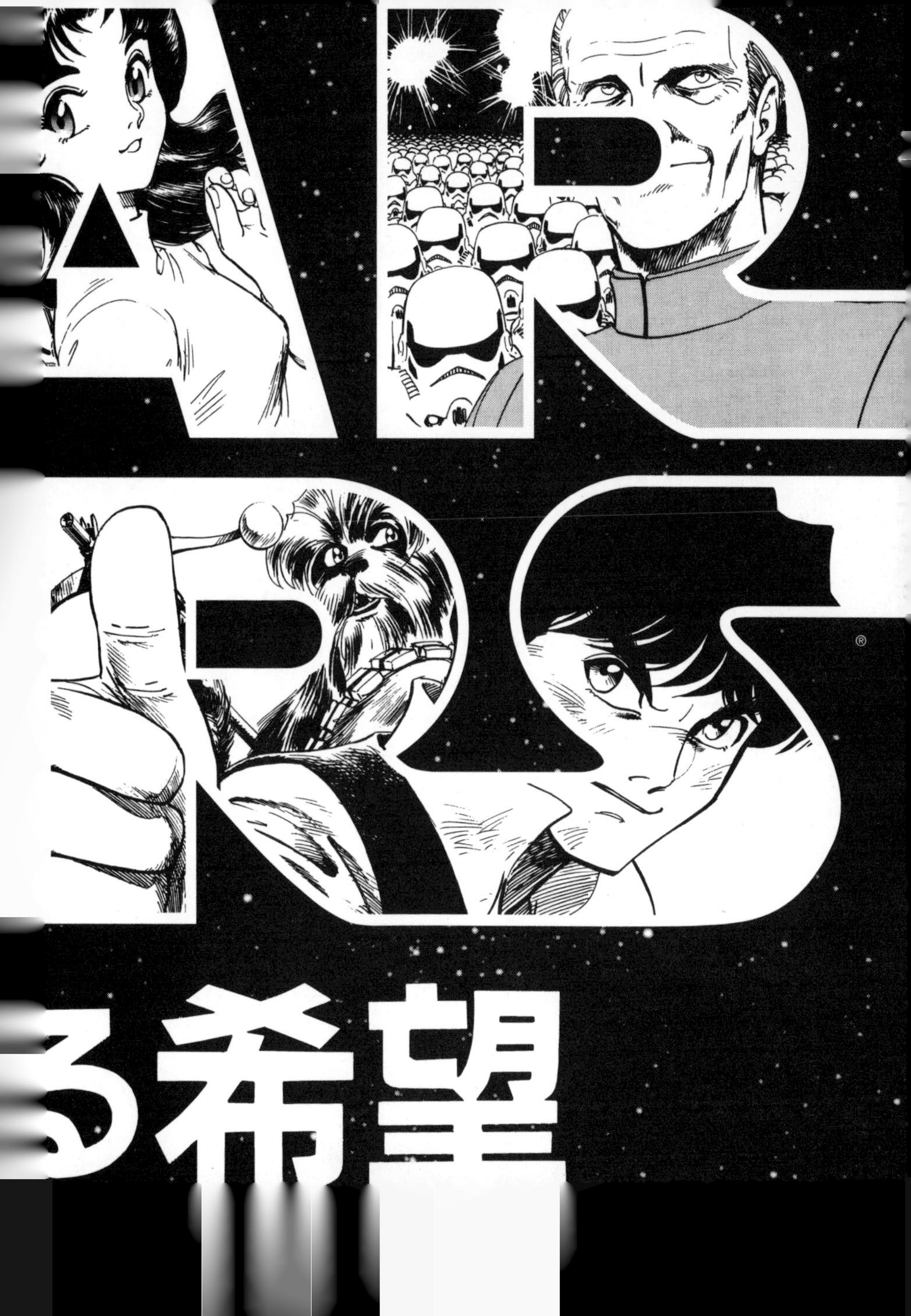
る希望

Episode IV

A NEW HOPE

It is a period of civil war. Rebel spaceships, striking from a hidden base, have won their first victory against the evil Galactic Empire.

During the battle, Rebel spies managed to steal secret plans to the Empire's ultimate weapon, the DEATH STAR, an armored space station with enough power to destroy an entire planet.

Pursued by the Empire's sinister agents, Princess Leia races home aboard her starship, custodian of the stolen plans that can save her people and restore freedom to the galaxy....

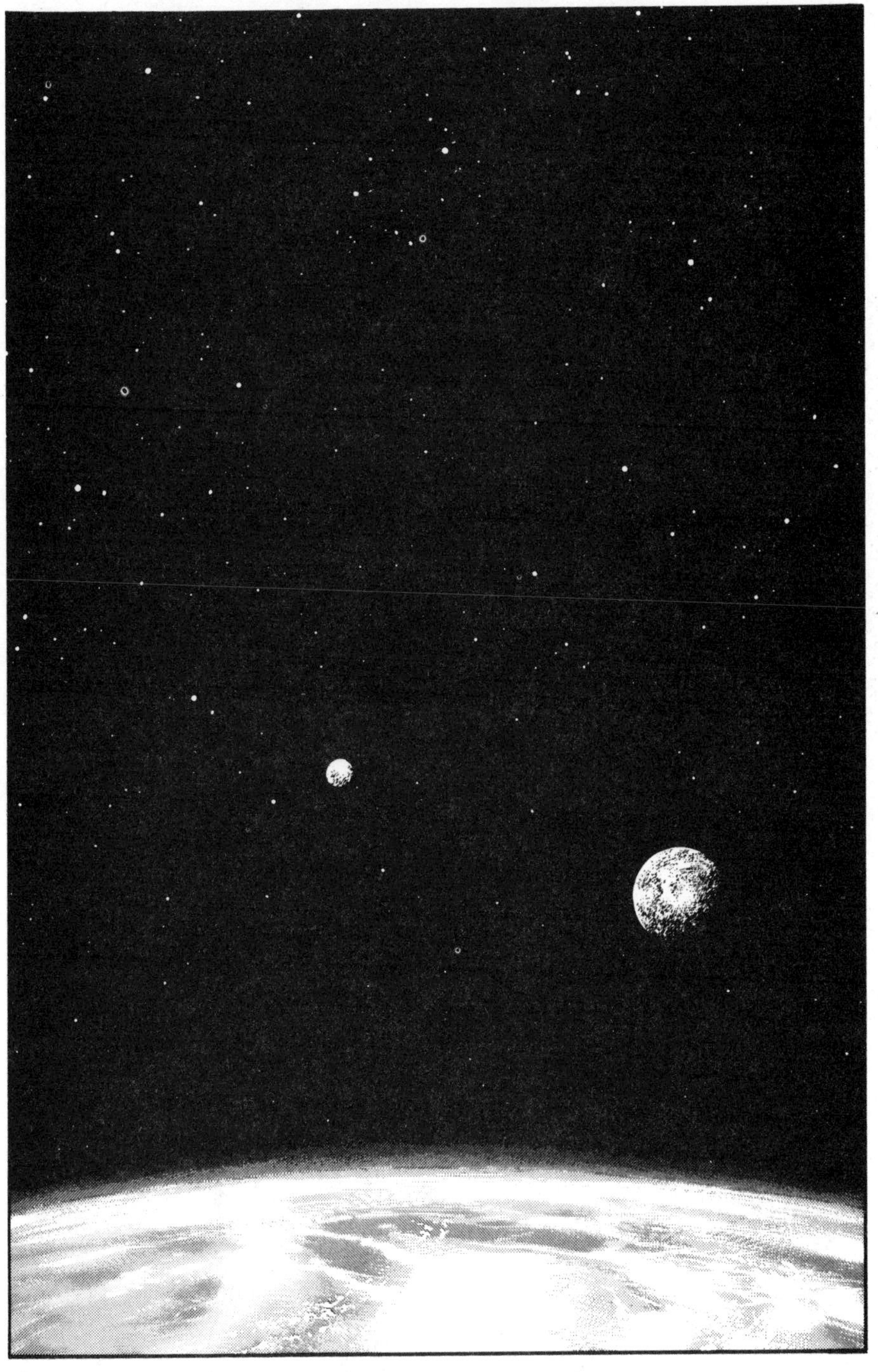

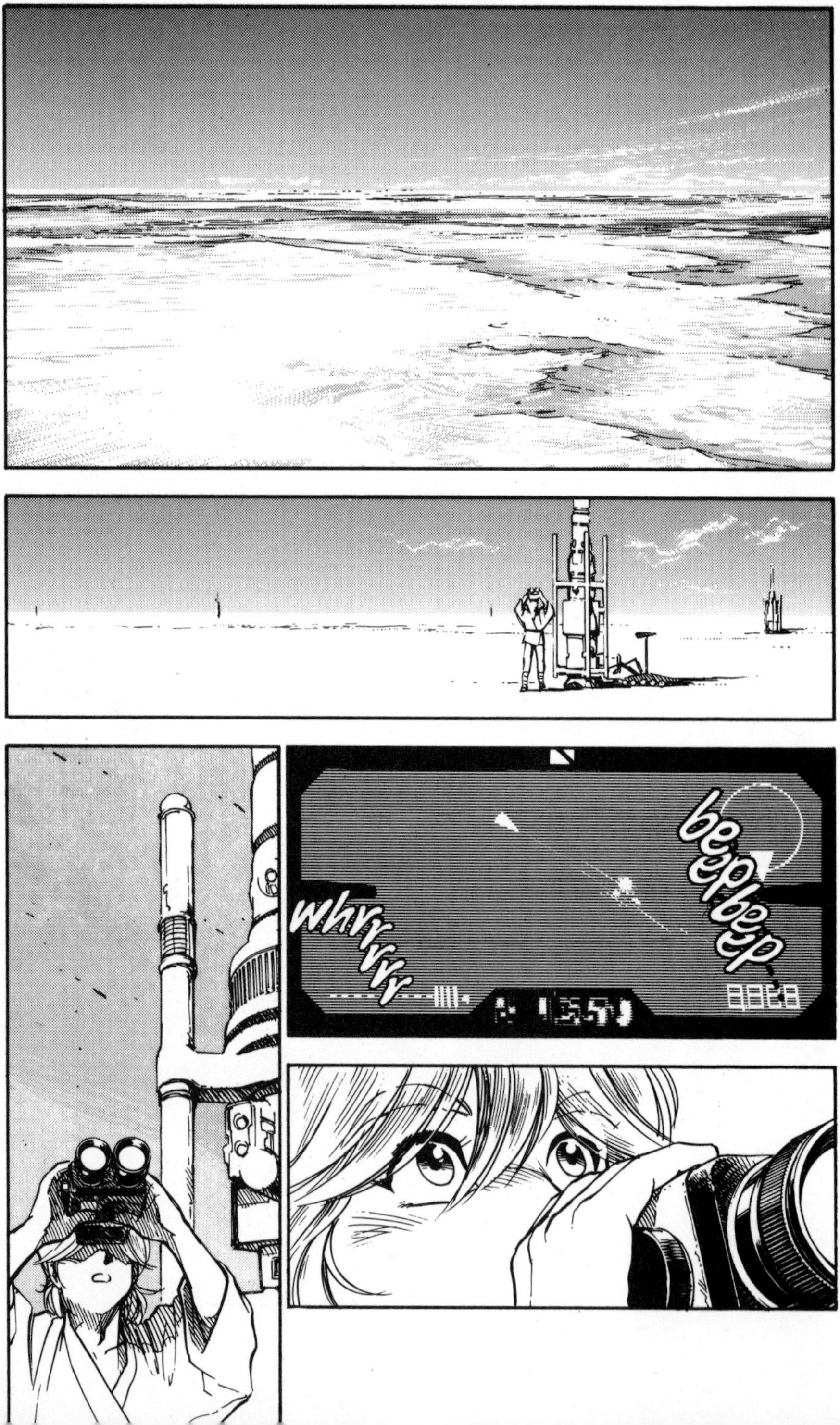
whrrrrr
beepbeep

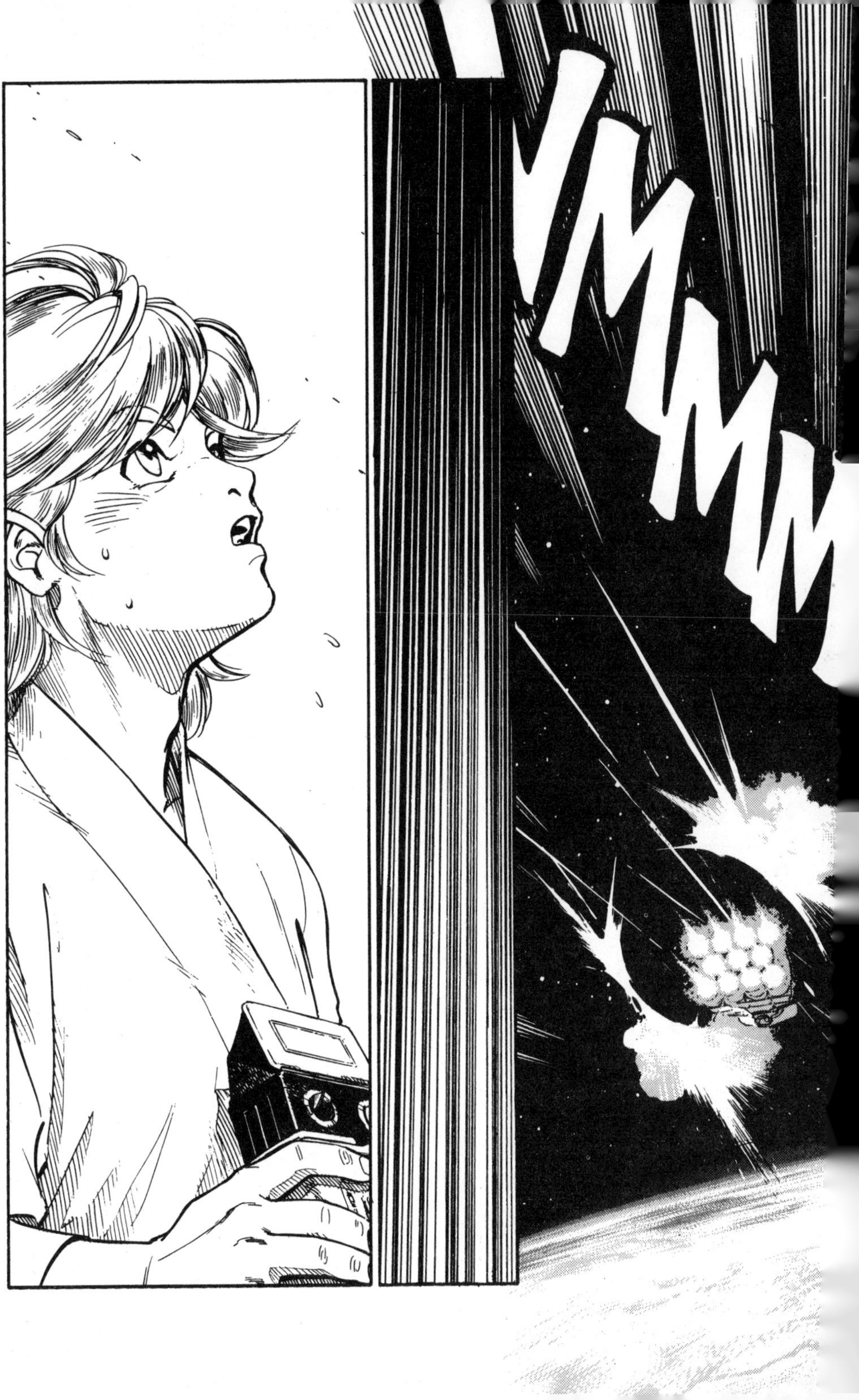

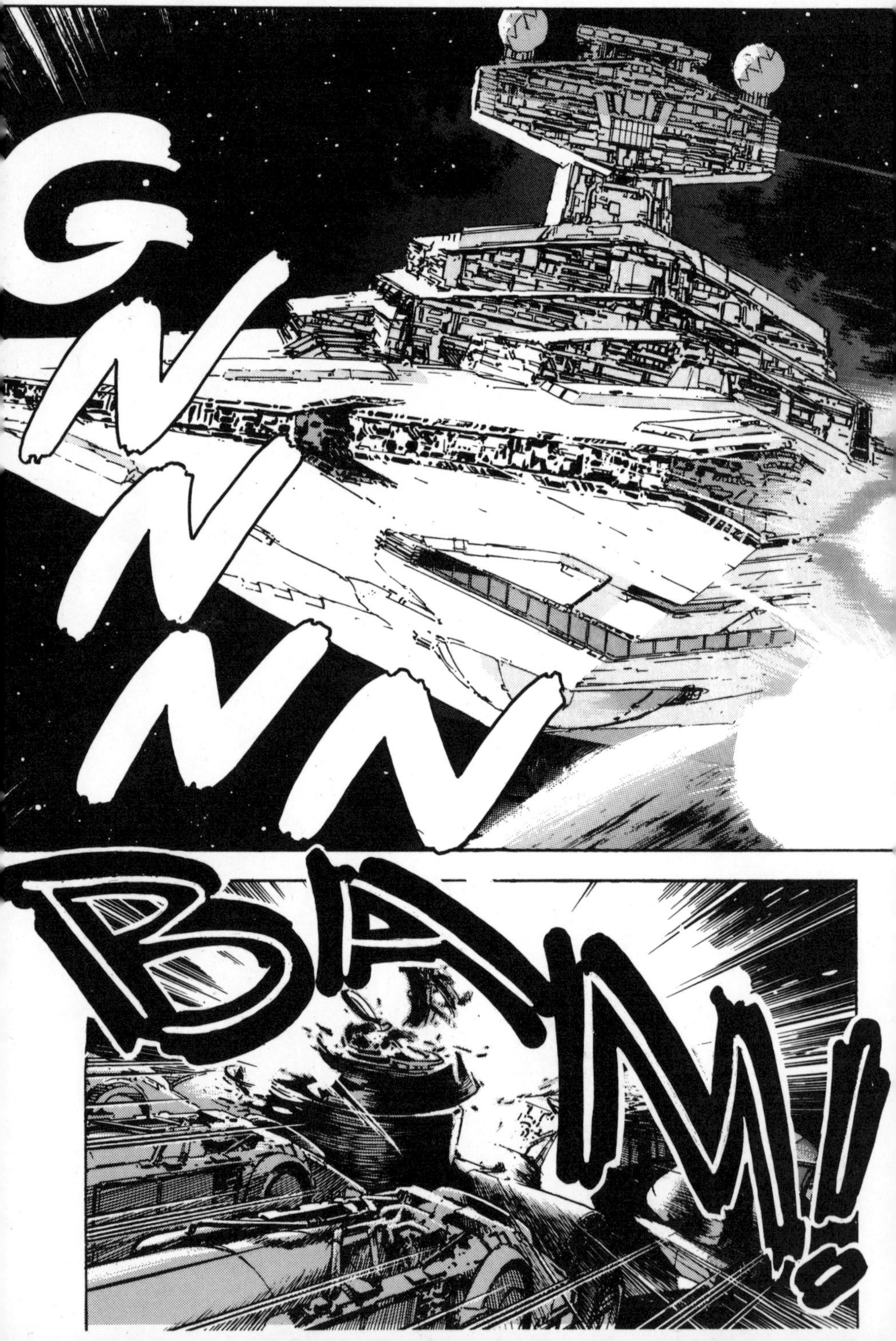
GNNNN
BAM!!

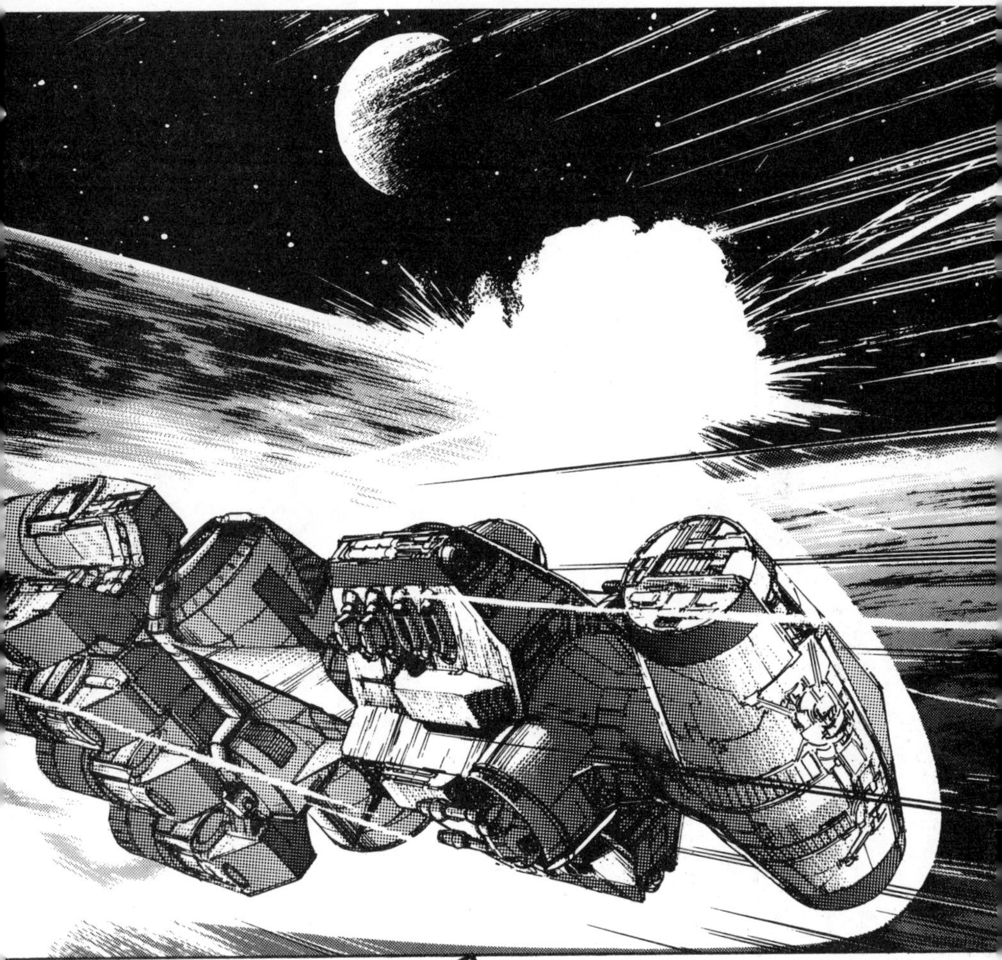

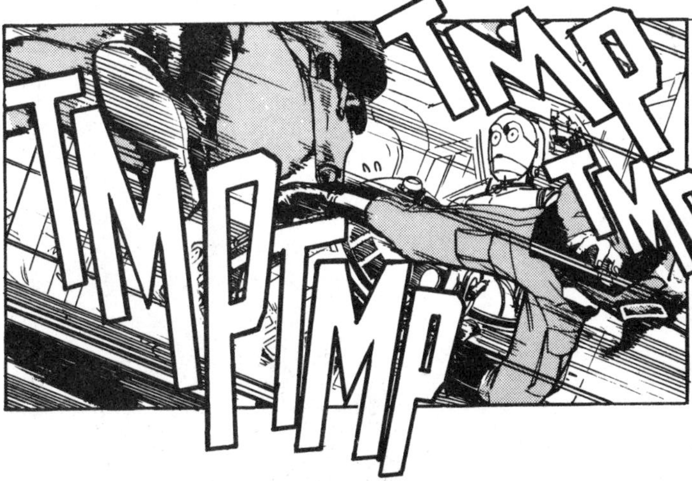
TMP
TMP
TMP
TMP
TMP

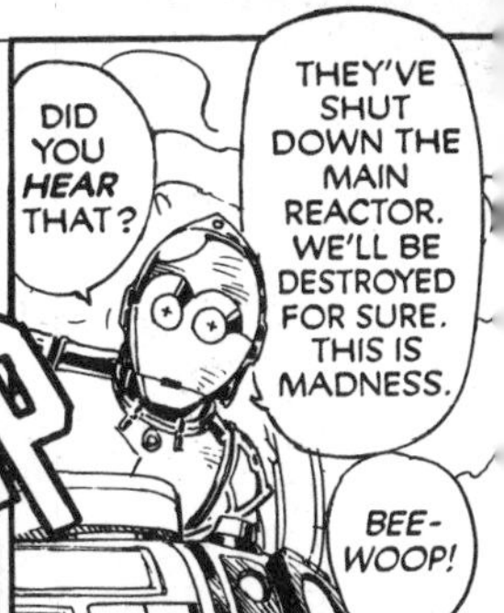
DID YOU *HEAR* THAT?
THEY'VE SHUT DOWN THE MAIN REACTOR. WE'LL BE DESTROYED FOR SURE. THIS IS MADNESS.
BEE-WOOP!

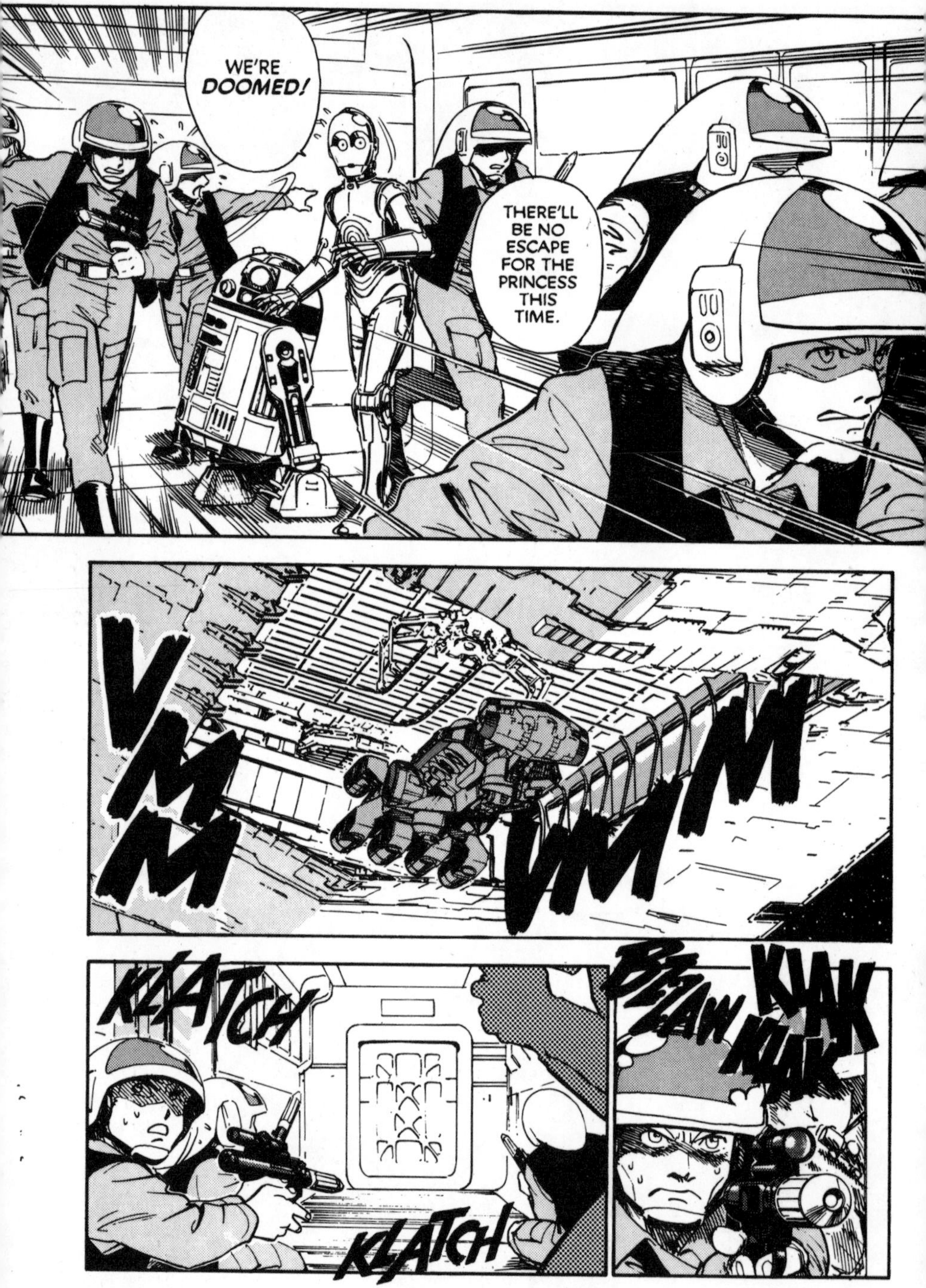
WE'RE **DOOMED!**
THERE'LL BE NO ESCAPE FOR THE PRINCESS THIS TIME.
VMM
VMMM
KLATCH
KLATCH
BZLAW
KLAK
KLAK

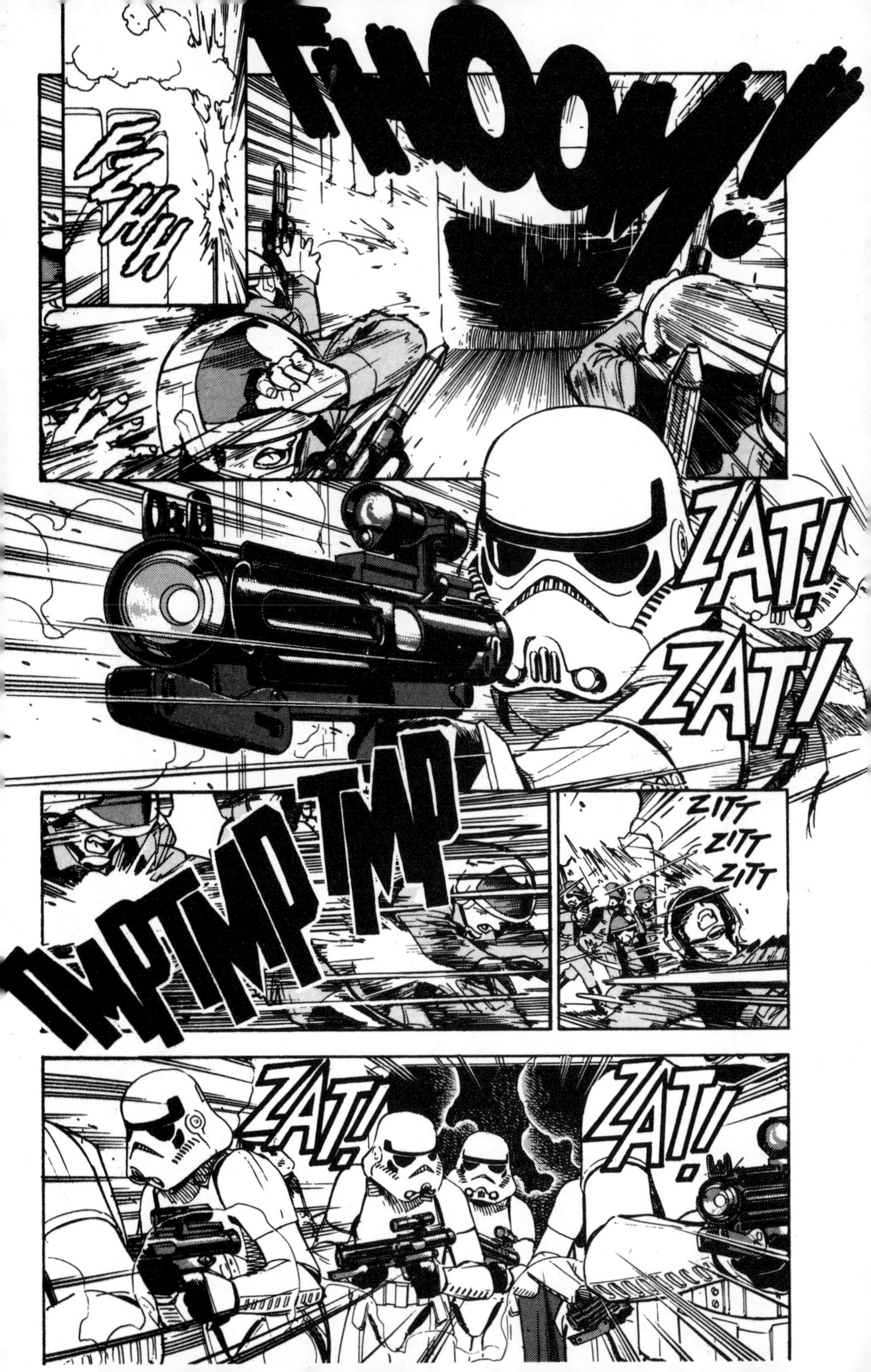
THOOM!!
ZAT! ZAT!
TMP TMP TMP TMP
ZITT
ZITT
ZITT
ZAT!
ZAT!

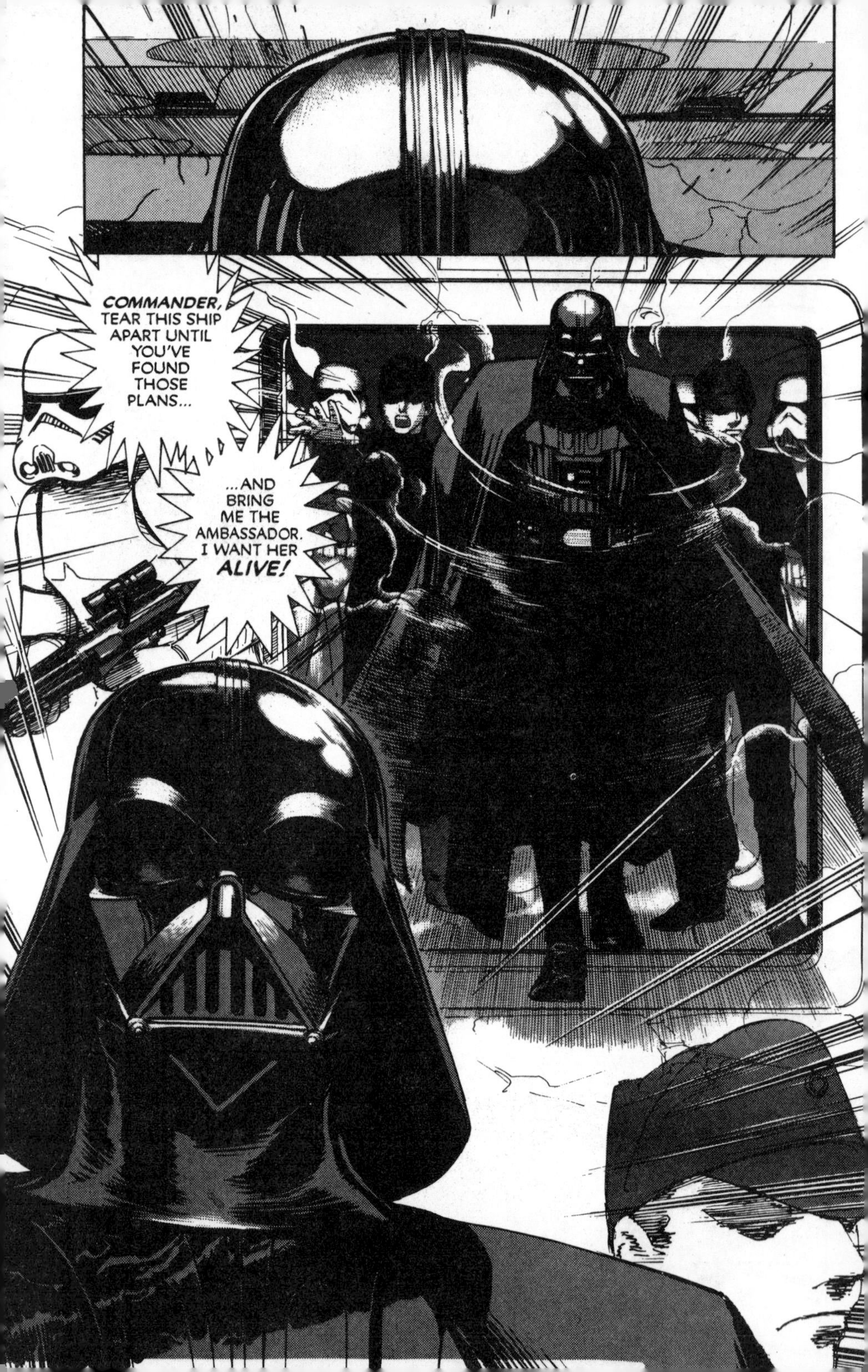
COMMANDER, TEAR THIS SHIP APART UNTIL YOU'VE FOUND THOSE PLANS...
...AND BRING ME THE AMBASSADOR. I WANT HER ALIVE!

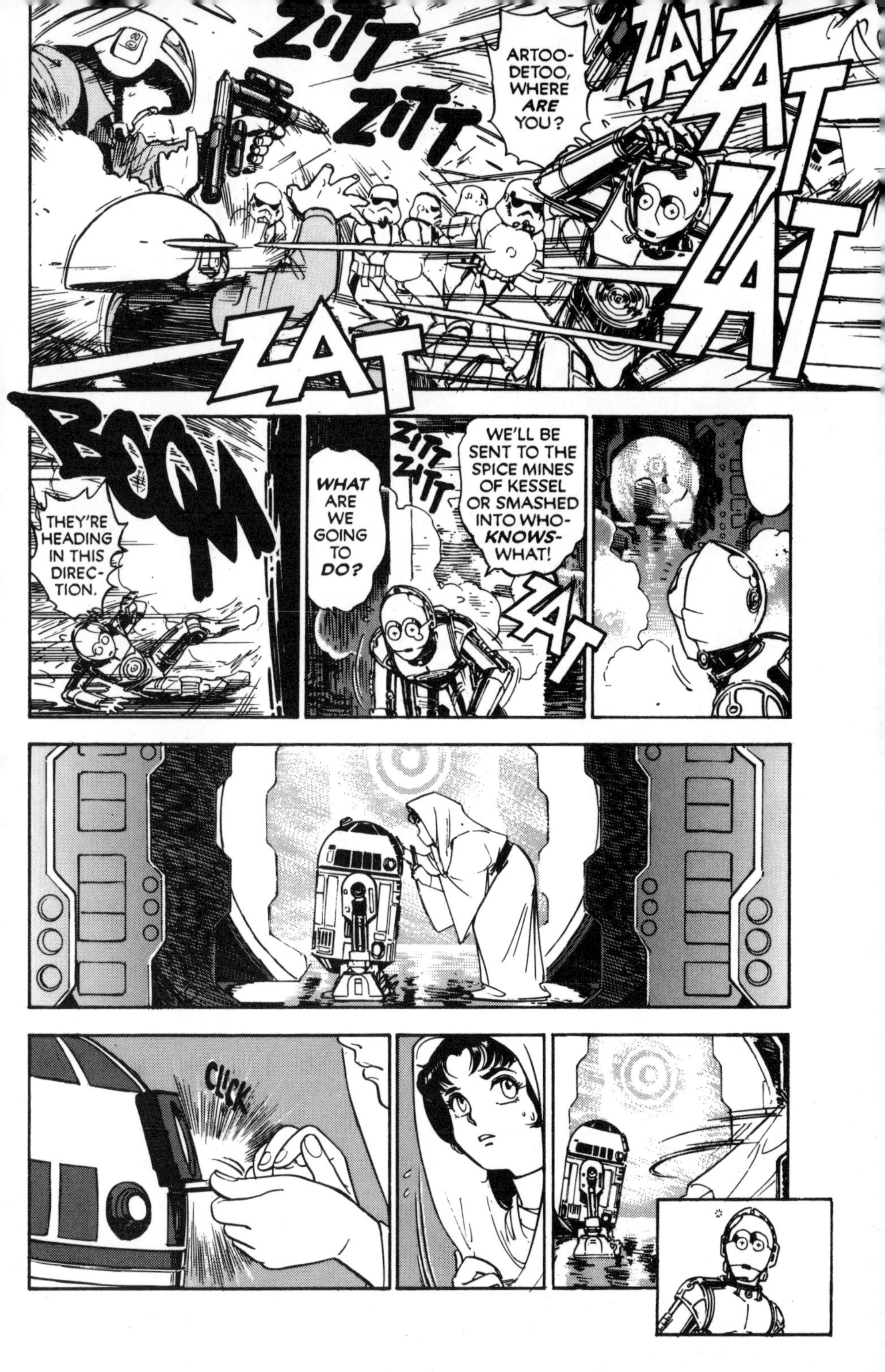
ZITT
ZITT
ARTOO-DETOO, WHERE *ARE* YOU?
ZAT
ZAT
ZAT
ZAT
BOOM
THEY'RE HEADING IN THIS DIRECTION.
ZITT ZITT
WHAT ARE WE GOING TO *DO?*
WE'LL BE SENT TO THE SPICE MINES OF KESSEL OR SMASHED INTO WHO-*KNOWS*-WHAT!
ZAT
CLICK

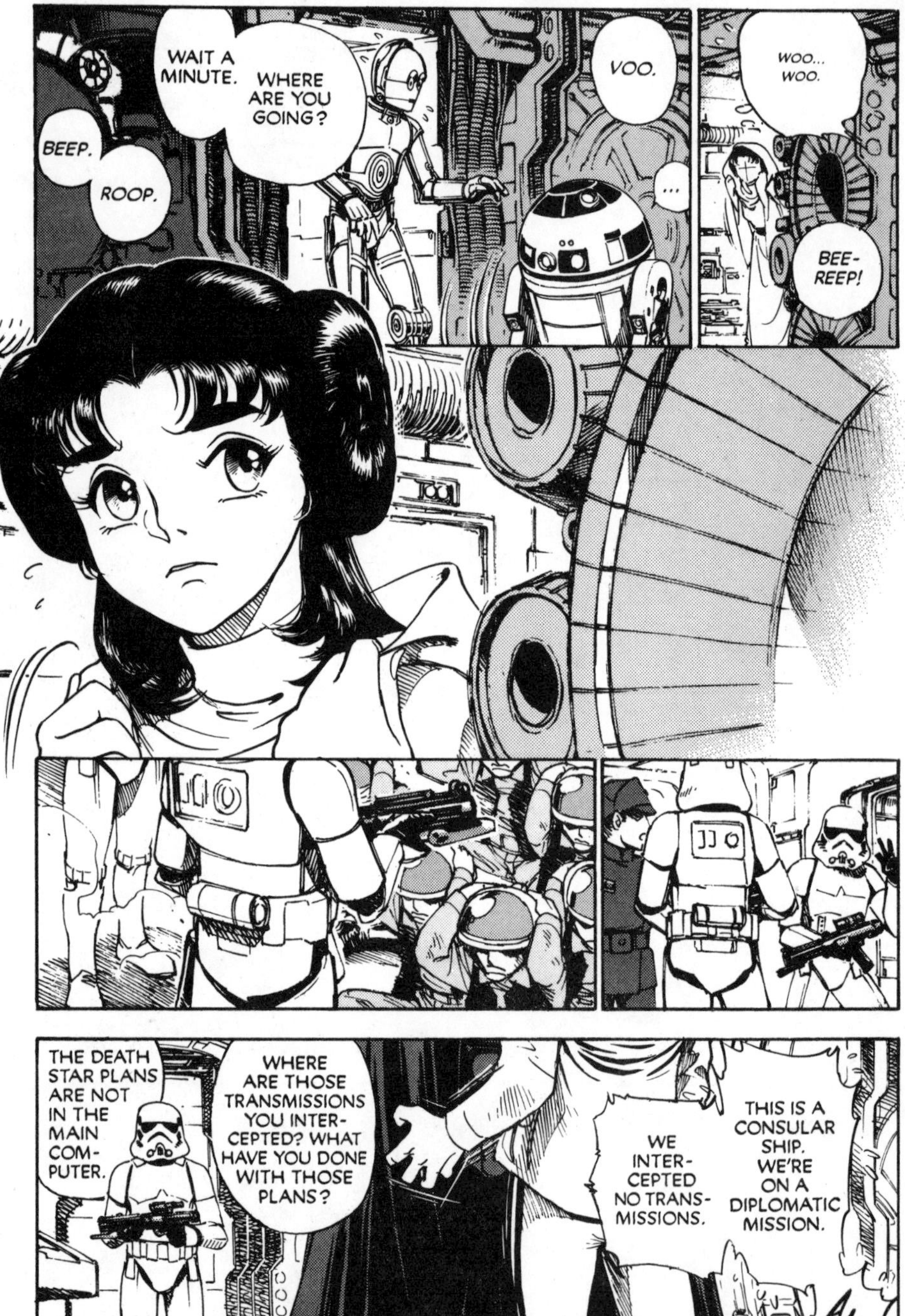
WAIT A MINUTE.
WHERE ARE YOU GOING?
BEEP.
ROOP.
VOO.
...
WOO... WOO.
BEE-REEP!
THE DEATH STAR PLANS ARE NOT IN THE MAIN COM-PUTER.
WHERE ARE THOSE TRANSMISSIONS YOU INTER-CEPTED? WHAT HAVE YOU DONE WITH THOSE PLANS?
WE INTER-CEPTED NO TRANS-MISSIONS.
THIS IS A CONSULAR SHIP. WE'RE ON A DIPLOMATIC MISSION.
AAAH...

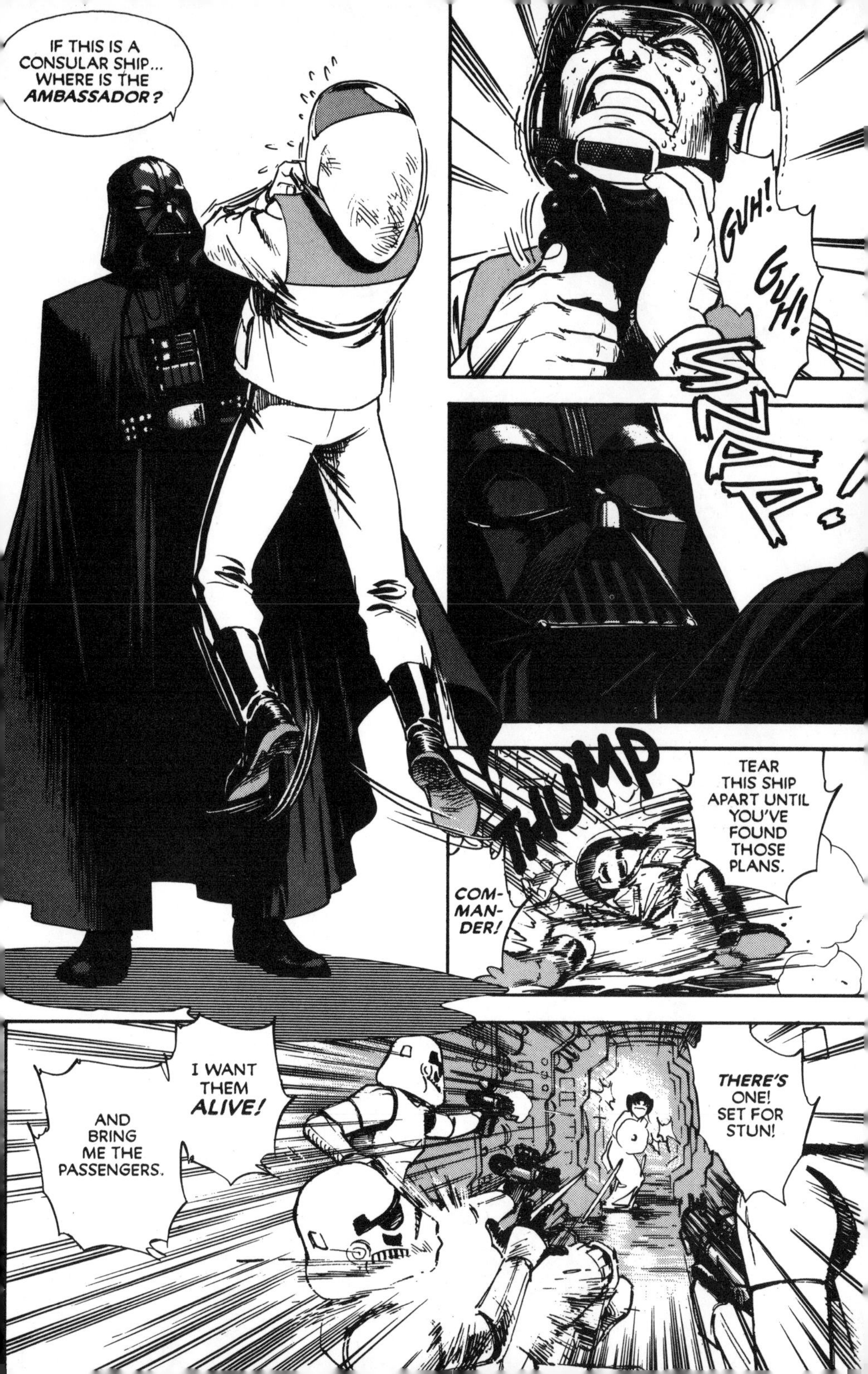
IF THIS IS A CONSULAR SHIP... WHERE IS THE AMBASSADOR?
GUH!
GUH!
SZZAA!
THUMP
COM-MAN-DER!
TEAR THIS SHIP APART UNTIL YOU'VE FOUND THOSE PLANS.
AND BRING ME THE PASSENGERS.
I WANT THEM ALIVE!
THERE'S ONE! SET FOR STUN!

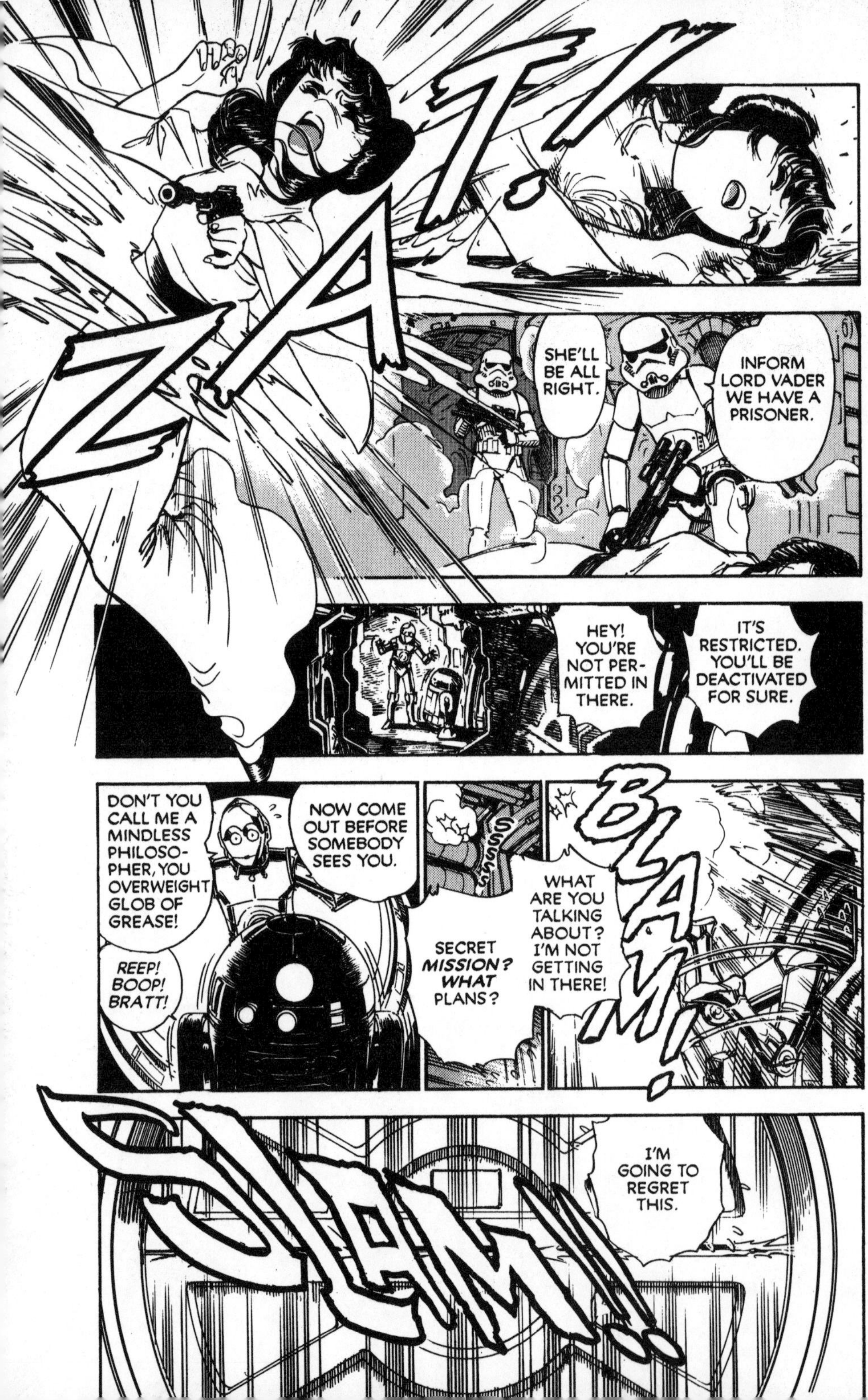
ZAT!
SHE'LL BE ALL RIGHT.
INFORM LORD VADER WE HAVE A PRISONER.
HEY! YOU'RE NOT PERMITTED IN THERE.
IT'S RESTRICTED. YOU'LL BE DEACTIVATED FOR SURE.
DON'T YOU CALL ME A MINDLESS PHILOSOPHER, YOU OVERWEIGHT GLOB OF GREASE!
NOW COME OUT BEFORE SOMEBODY SEES YOU.
REEP! BOOP! BRATT!
SSSSS
SECRET ***MISSION? WHAT*** PLANS?
BLAM!
WHAT ARE YOU TALKING ABOUT? I'M NOT GETTING IN THERE!
SLAM!!
I'M GOING TO REGRET THIS.

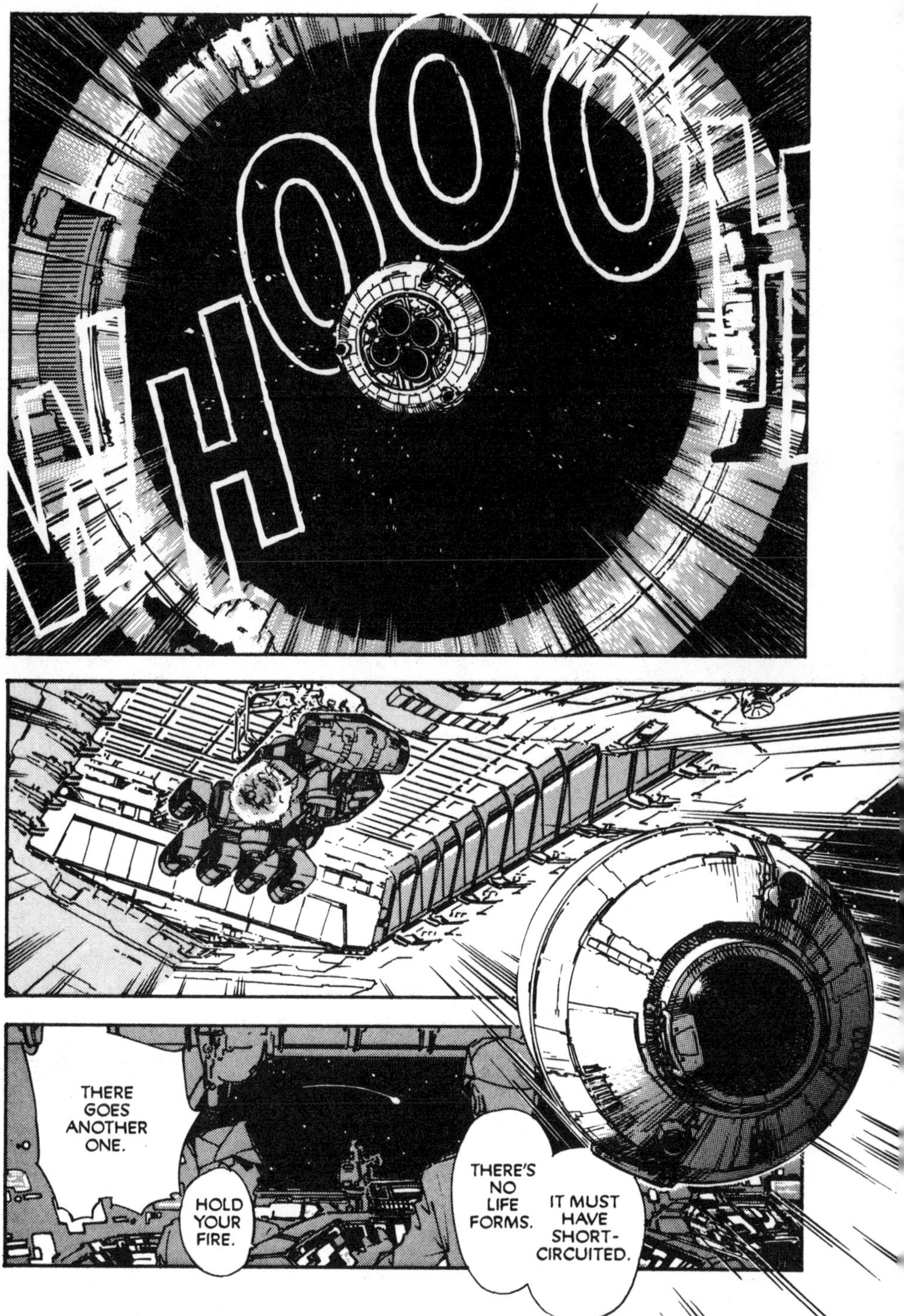
WHOOO
THERE GOES ANOTHER ONE.
HOLD YOUR FIRE.
THERE'S NO LIFE FORMS.
IT MUST HAVE SHORT-CIRCUITED.

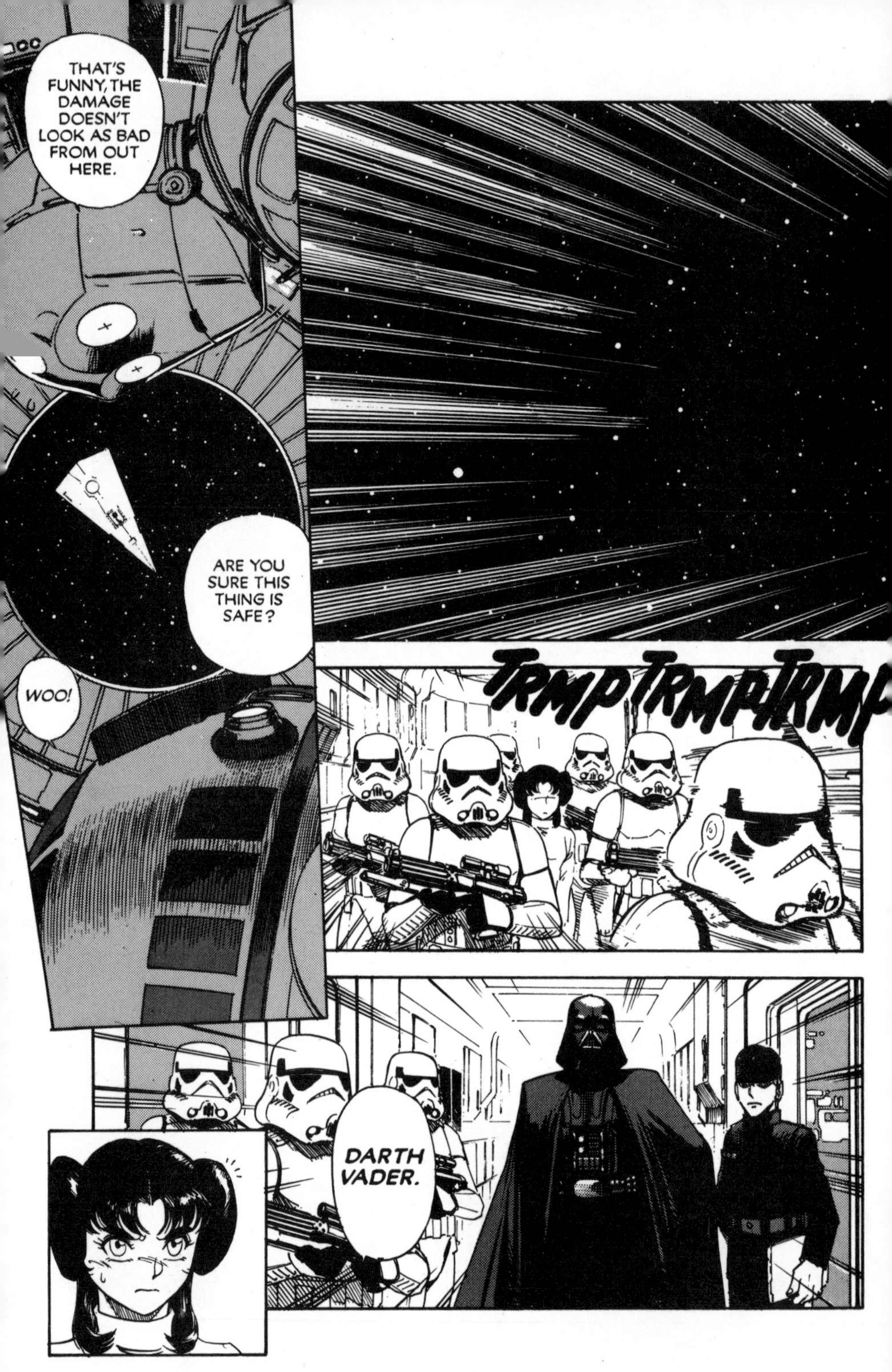
THAT'S FUNNY, THE DAMAGE DOESN'T LOOK AS BAD FROM OUT HERE.
ARE YOU SURE THIS THING IS SAFE?
WOO!
TRMP TRMP TRMP
DARTH VADER.

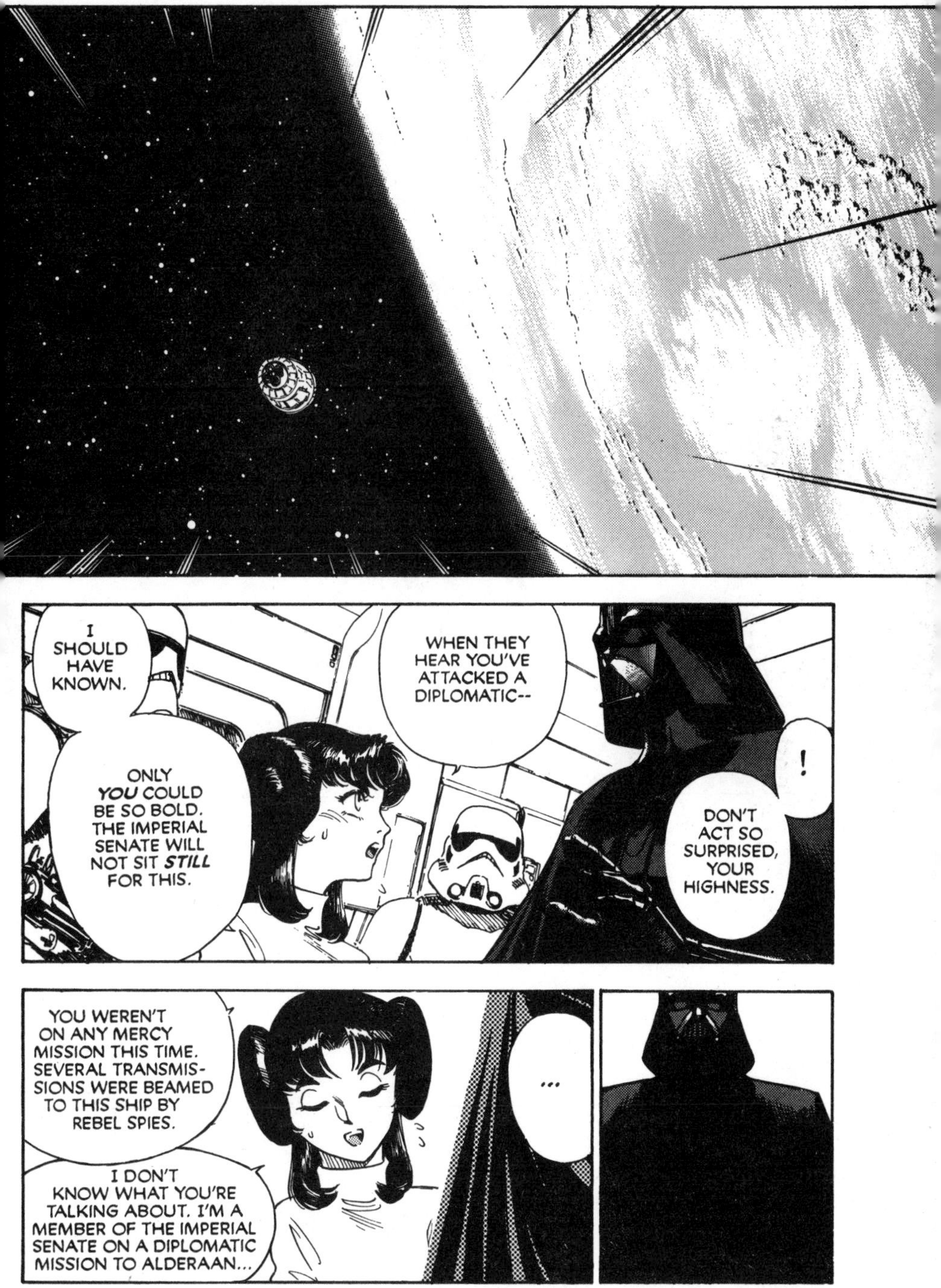
I SHOULD HAVE KNOWN.
ONLY *YOU* COULD BE SO BOLD. THE IMPERIAL SENATE WILL NOT SIT *STILL* FOR THIS.
WHEN THEY HEAR YOU'VE ATTACKED A DIPLOMATIC--
!
DON'T ACT SO SURPRISED, YOUR HIGHNESS.
YOU WEREN'T ON ANY MERCY MISSION THIS TIME. SEVERAL TRANSMISSIONS WERE BEAMED TO THIS SHIP BY REBEL SPIES.
I DON'T KNOW WHAT YOU'RE TALKING ABOUT. I'M A MEMBER OF THE IMPERIAL SENATE ON A DIPLOMATIC MISSION TO ALDERAAN...
...

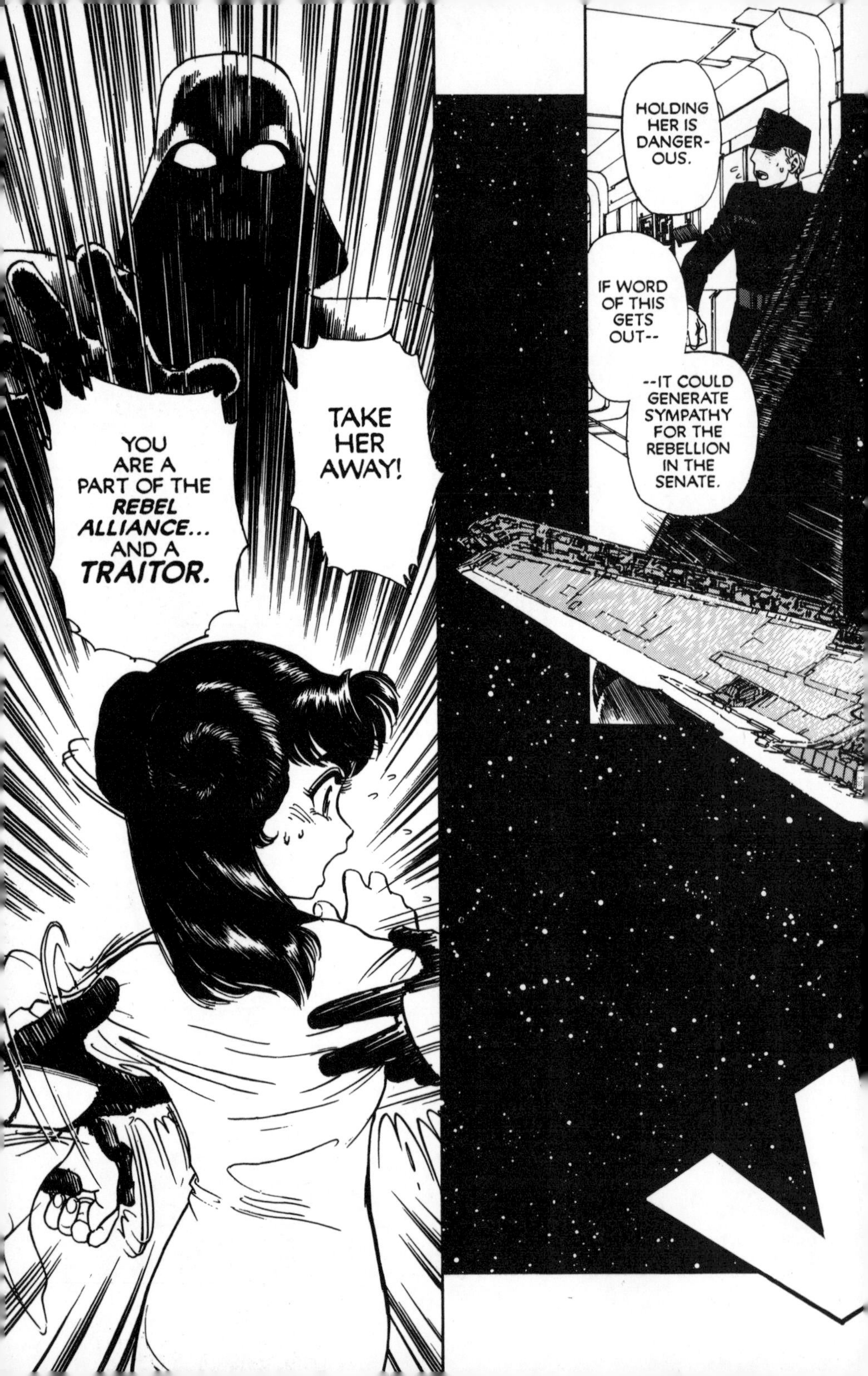
YOU ARE A PART OF THE *REBEL ALLIANCE*... AND A ***TRAITOR.***
TAKE HER AWAY!
HOLDING HER IS DANGER-OUS.
IF WORD OF THIS GETS OUT--
--IT COULD GENERATE SYMPATHY FOR THE REBELLION IN THE SENATE.

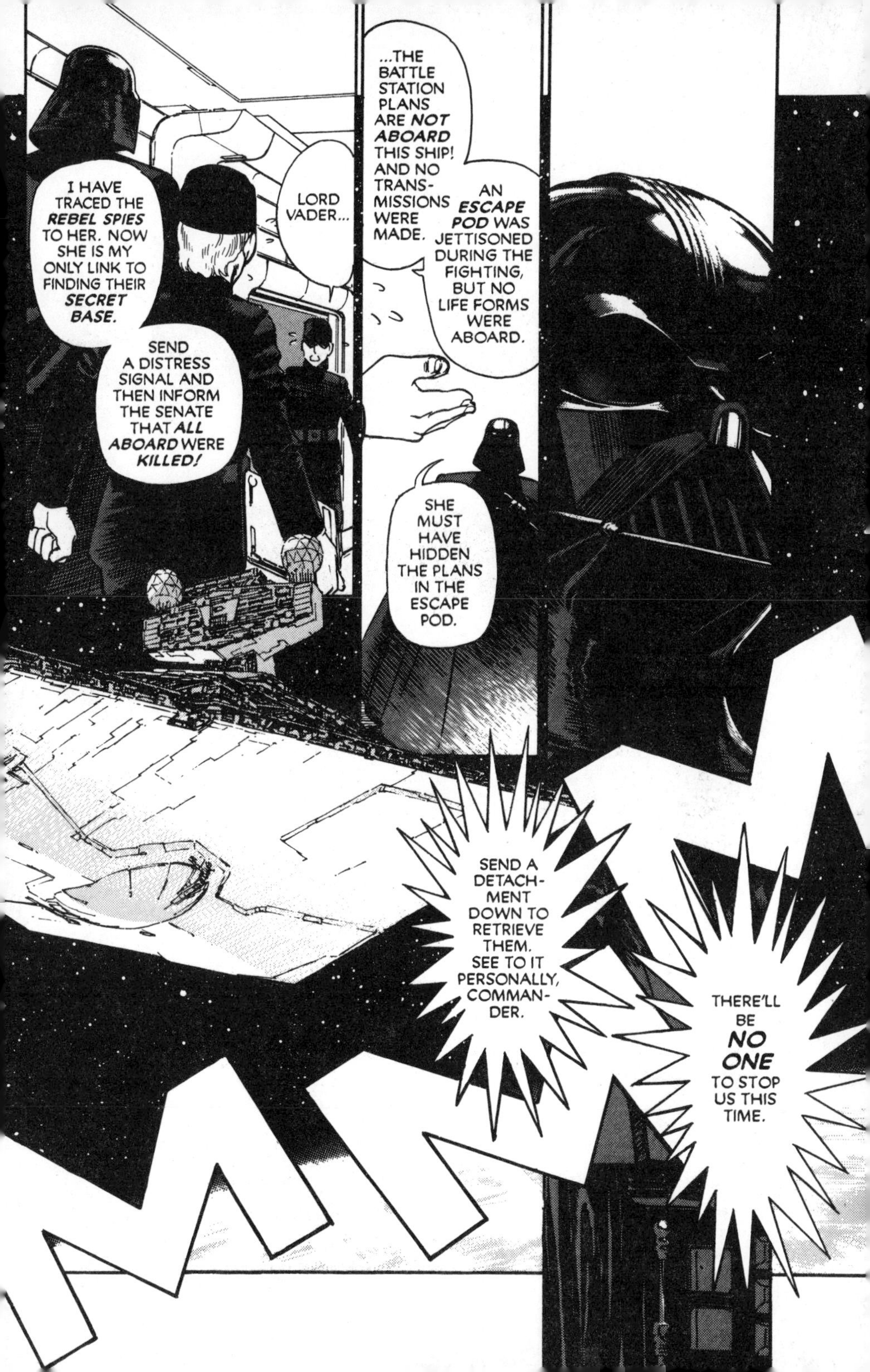
I HAVE TRACED THE *REBEL SPIES* TO HER. NOW SHE IS MY ONLY LINK TO FINDING THEIR *SECRET BASE.*
SEND A DISTRESS SIGNAL AND THEN INFORM THE SENATE THAT *ALL ABOARD* WERE *KILLED!*
LORD VADER...
...THE BATTLE STATION PLANS ARE *NOT ABOARD* THIS SHIP! AND NO TRANS-MISSIONS WERE MADE.
AN *ESCAPE POD* WAS JETTISONED DURING THE FIGHTING, BUT NO LIFE FORMS WERE ABOARD.
SHE MUST HAVE HIDDEN THE PLANS IN THE ESCAPE POD.
SEND A DETACH-MENT DOWN TO RETRIEVE THEM. SEE TO IT PERSONALLY, COMMAN-DER.
THERE'LL BE ***NO ONE*** TO STOP US THIS TIME.

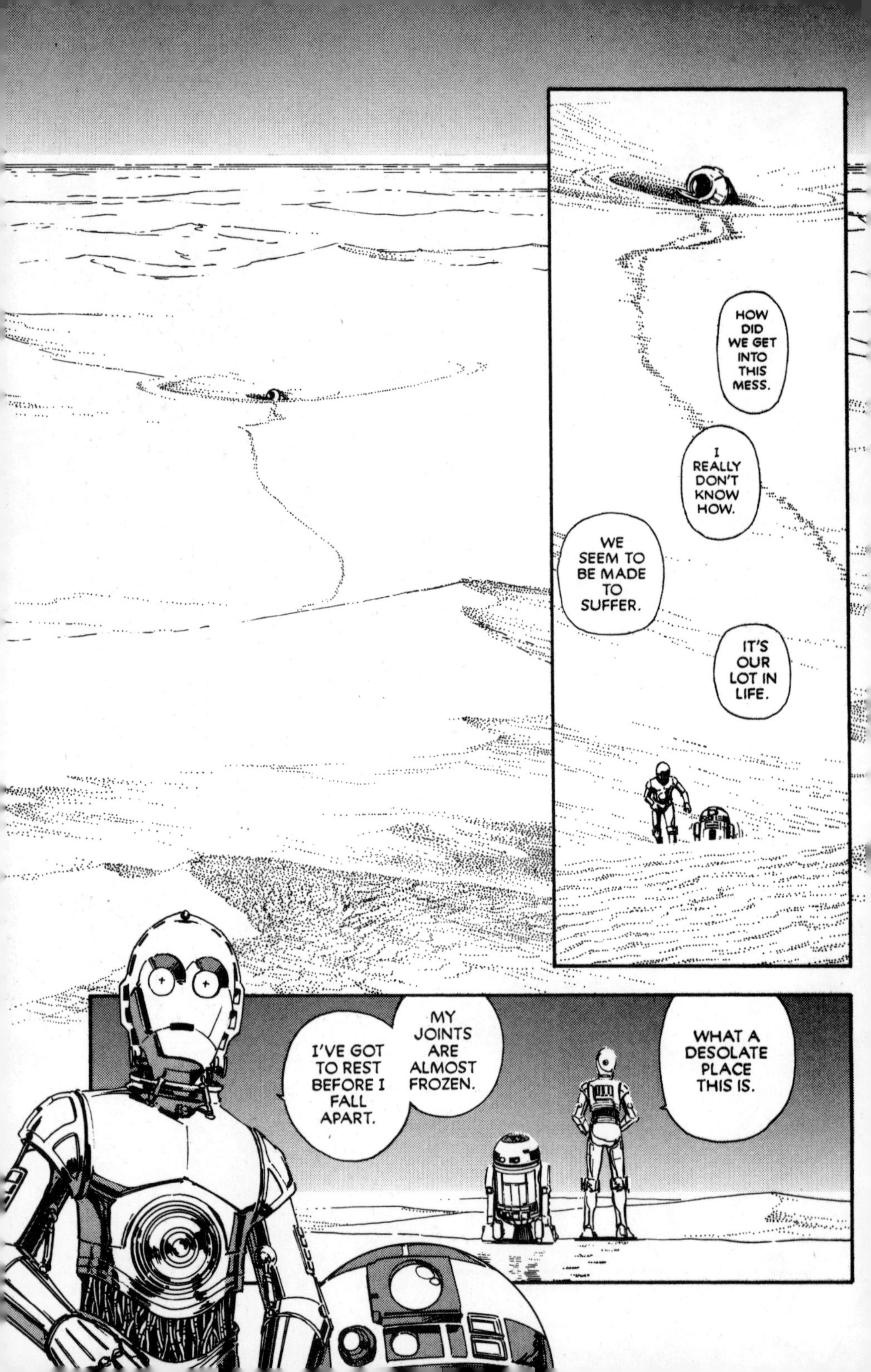
HOW DID WE GET INTO THIS MESS.
I REALLY DON'T KNOW HOW.
WE SEEM TO BE MADE TO SUFFER.
IT'S OUR LOT IN LIFE.
I'VE GOT TO REST BEFORE I FALL APART.
MY JOINTS ARE ALMOST FROZEN.
WHAT A DESOLATE PLACE THIS IS.

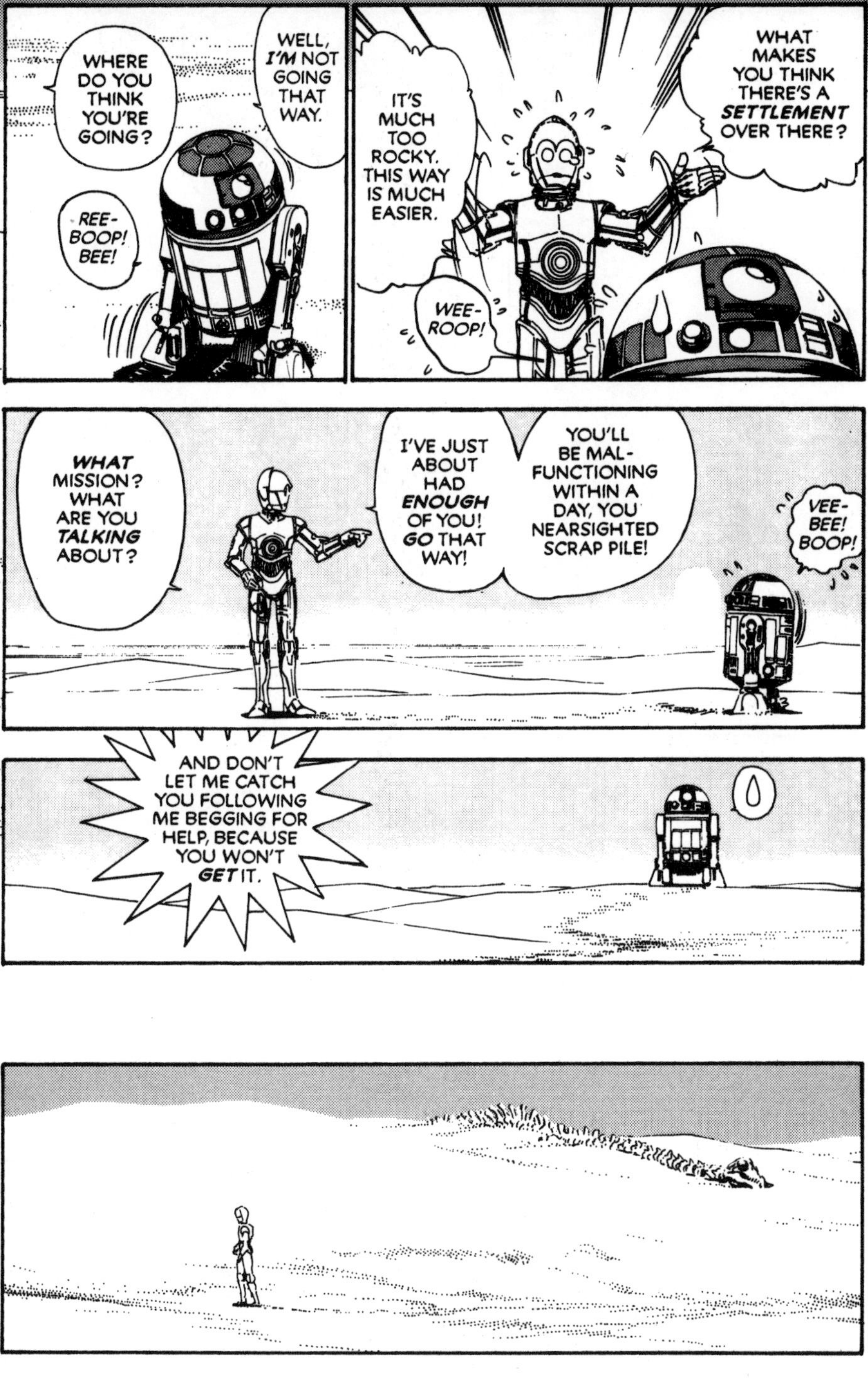
WHERE DO YOU THINK YOU'RE GOING?
WELL, *I'M* NOT GOING THAT WAY.
REE-BOOP! BEE!
IT'S MUCH TOO ROCKY. THIS WAY IS MUCH EASIER.
WHAT MAKES YOU THINK THERE'S A *SETTLEMENT* OVER THERE?
WEE-ROOP!
WHAT MISSION? WHAT ARE YOU *TALKING* ABOUT?
I'VE JUST ABOUT HAD *ENOUGH* OF YOU! *GO* THAT WAY!
YOU'LL BE MAL-FUNCTIONING WITHIN A DAY, YOU NEARSIGHTED SCRAP PILE!
VEE-BEE! BOOP!
AND DON'T LET ME CATCH YOU FOLLOWING ME BEGGING FOR HELP, BECAUSE YOU WON'T *GET* IT.

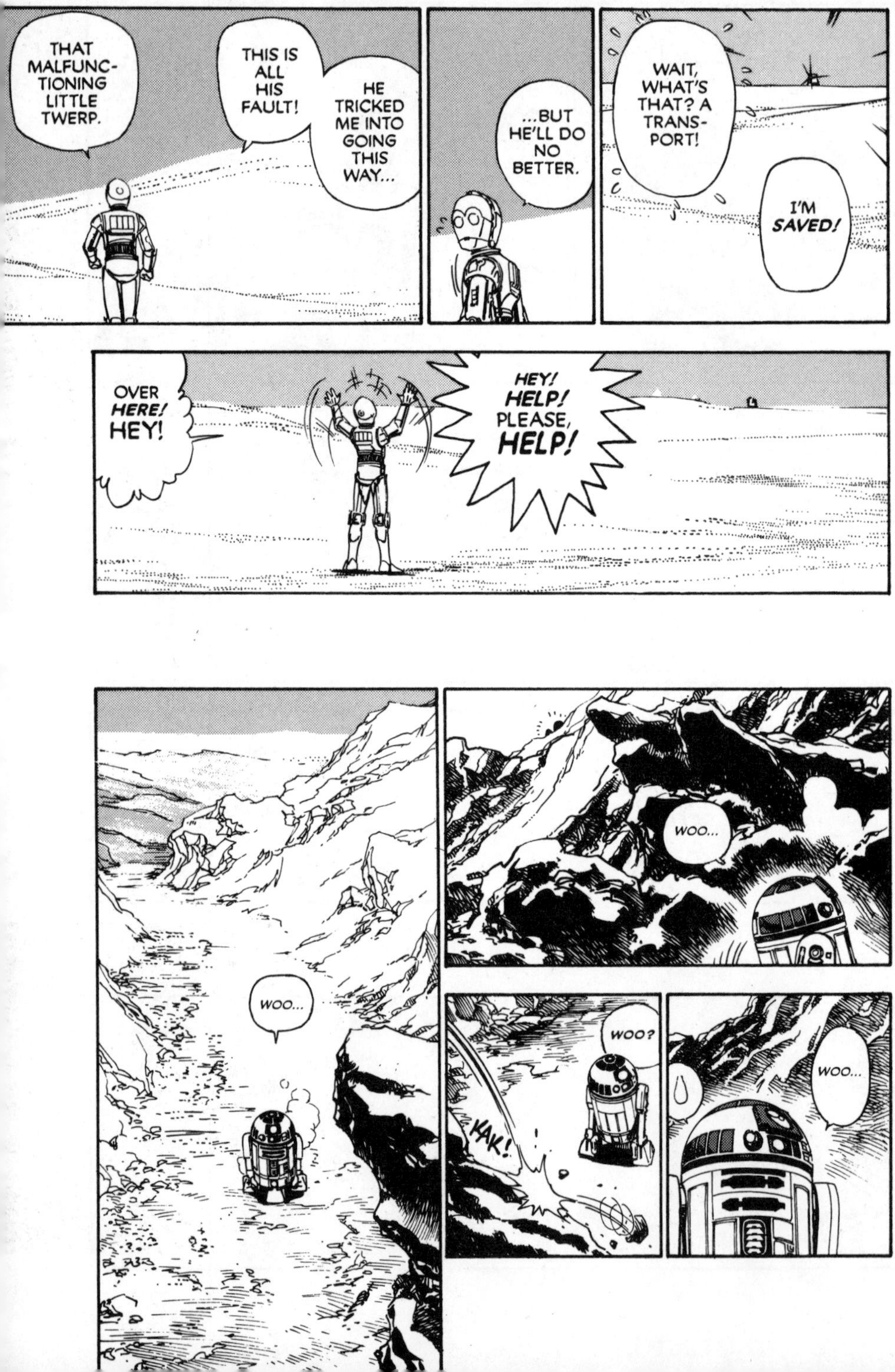
THAT MALFUNCTIONING LITTLE TWERP.
THIS IS ALL HIS FAULT!
HE TRICKED ME INTO GOING THIS WAY...
...BUT HE'LL DO NO BETTER.
WAIT, WHAT'S THAT? A TRANSPORT!
I'M *SAVED!*
OVER *HERE!* HEY!
HEY! HELP! PLEASE, *HELP!*
WOO...
WOO...
WOO?
KAK!
WOO...

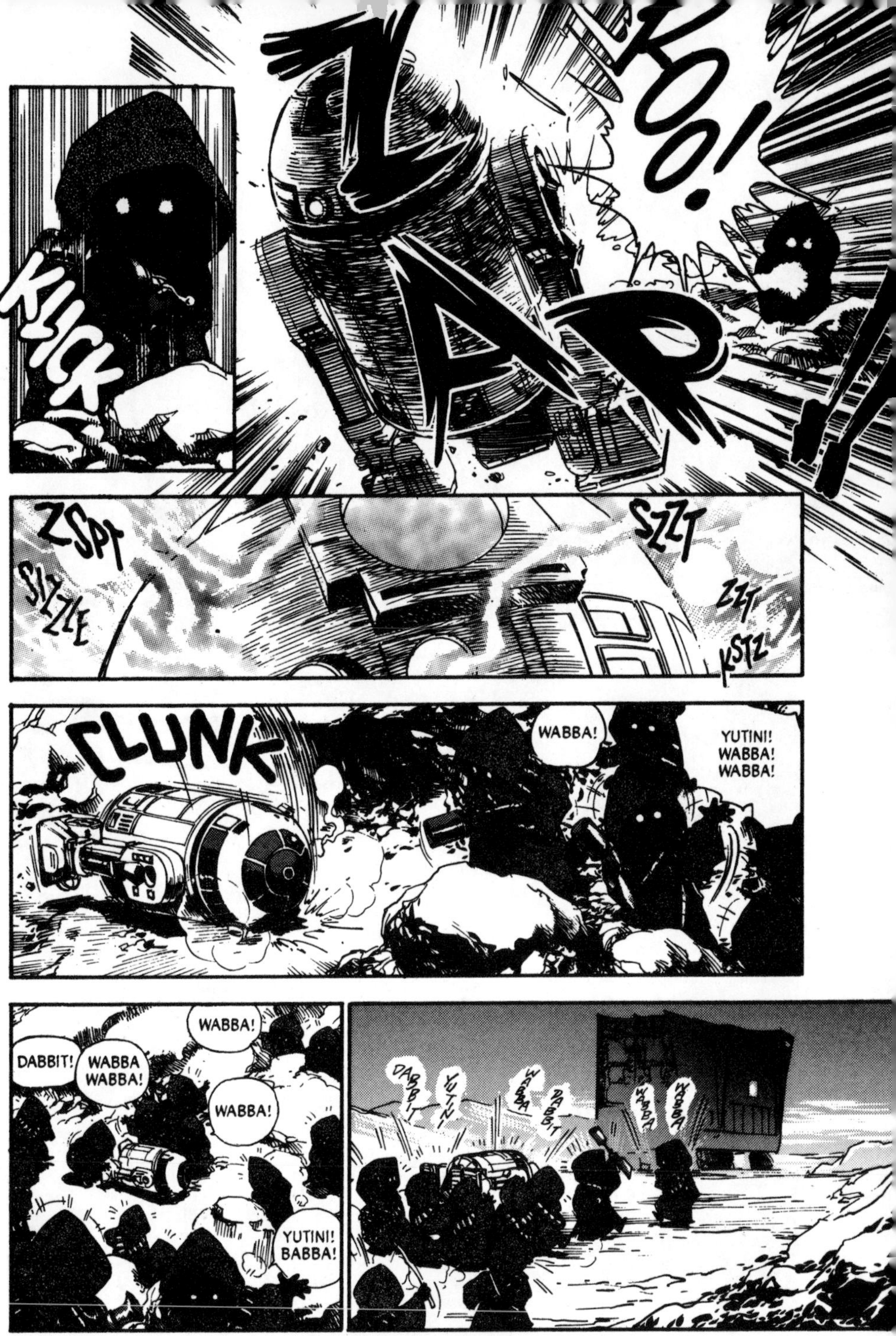
KLICK
ZAP!!
KOO!
ZSPT
SIZZLE
SZZT
ZZZT
KSTZ
CLUNK
WABBA!
YUTINI! WABBA! WABBA!
WABBA!
DABBIT!
WABBA WABBA!
WABBA!
YUTINI! BABBA!
DABBIT
YUTINI
WABBA
DABBIT
WABBA
WABBA

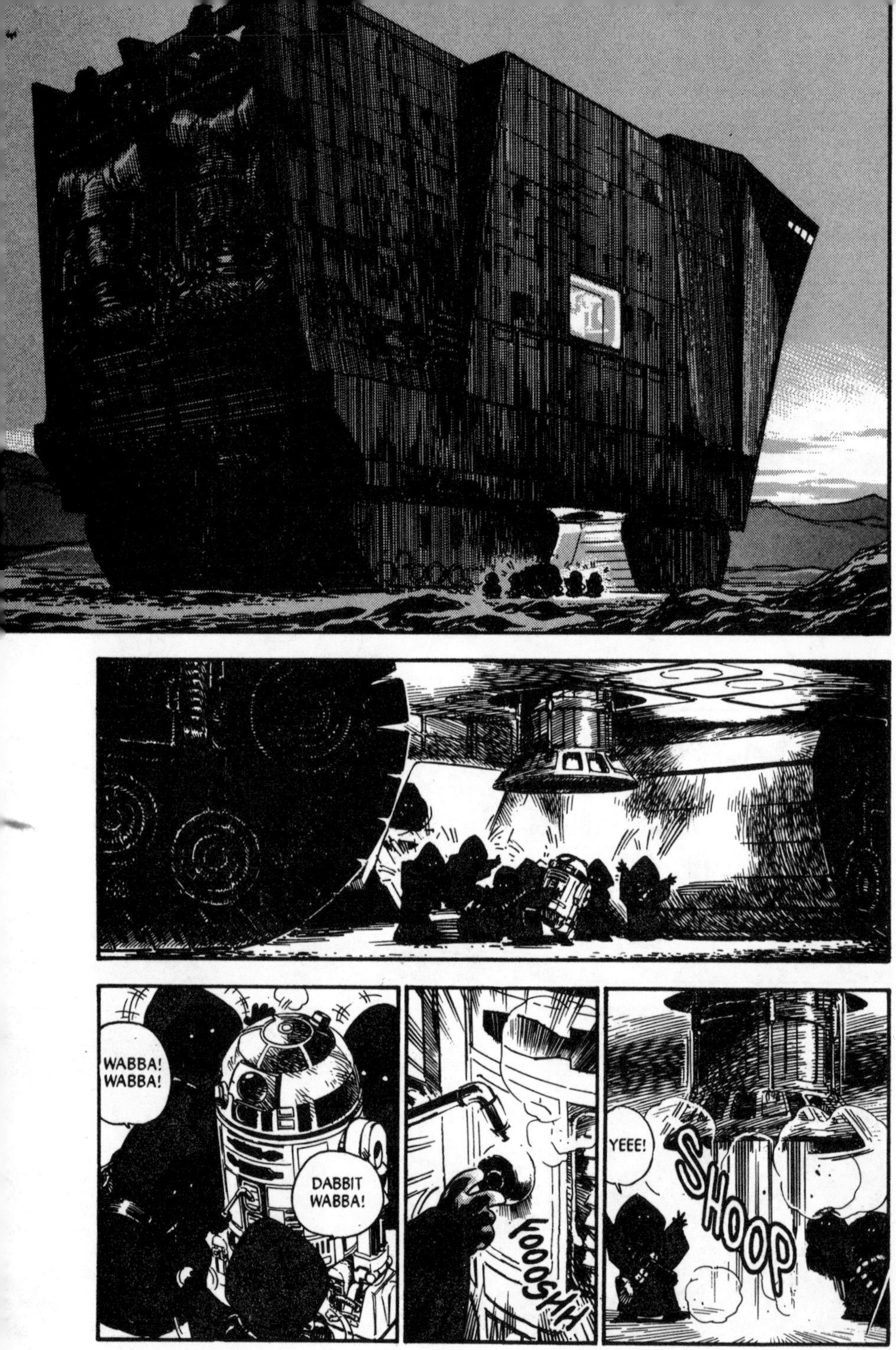
WABBA! WABBA!
DABBIT WABBA!
FOOOSHH
YEEE!
SHOOP

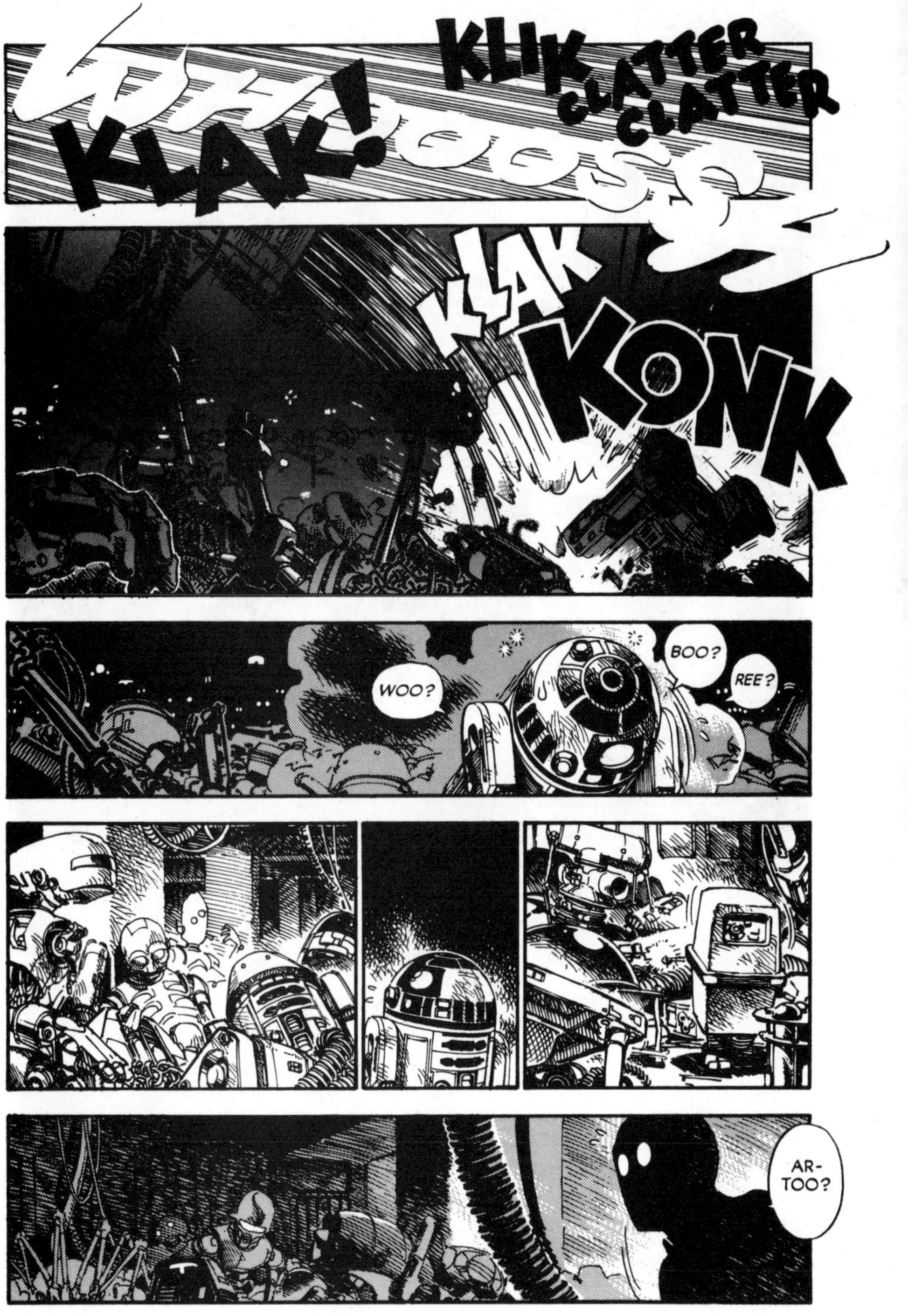
KLAK!
KLIK
CLATTER
CLATTER
KLAK
KONK
WOO?
BOO?
REE?
AR-
TOO?

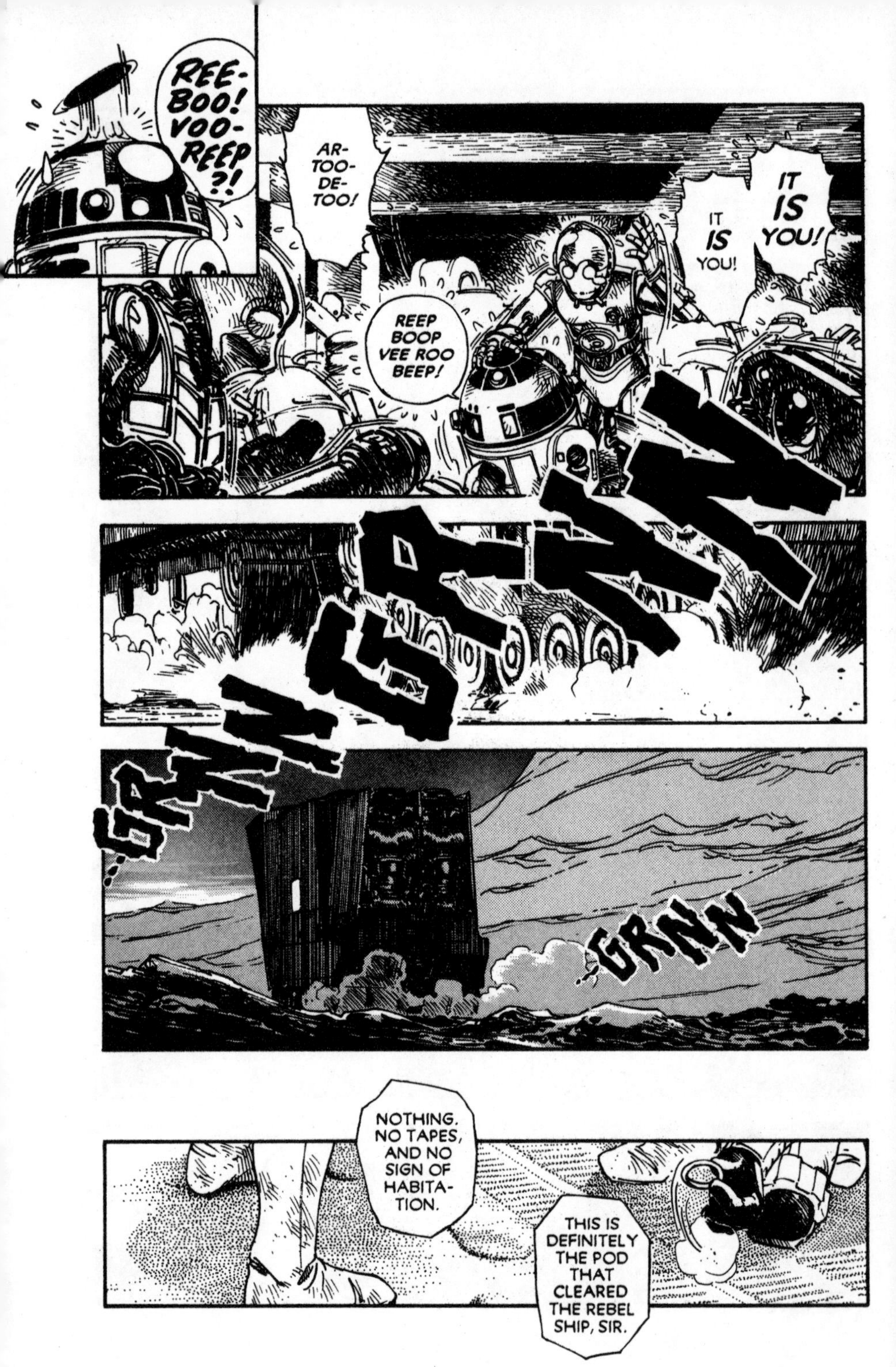

REE-BOO! VOO-REEP?!
ARTOO-DETOO!
IT IS YOU!
IT IS YOU!
REEP BOOP VEE ROO BEEP!
GRNN
GRNN
NOTHING. NO TAPES, AND NO SIGN OF HABITATION.
THIS IS DEFINITELY THE POD THAT CLEARED THE REBEL SHIP, SIR.

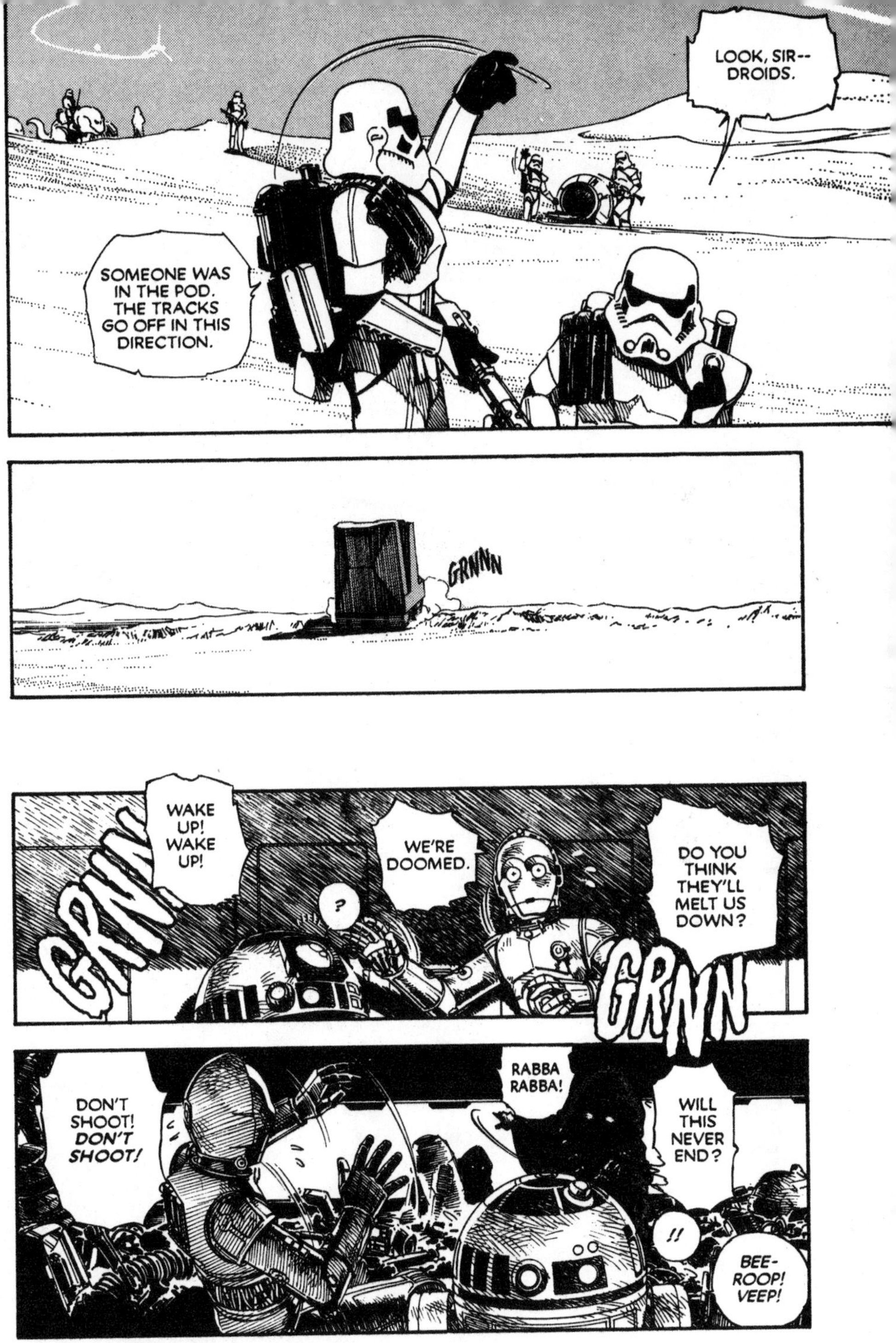
SOMEONE WAS IN THE POD. THE TRACKS GO OFF IN THIS DIRECTION.
LOOK, SIR-- DROIDS.
GRNNN
GRNN
WAKE UP! WAKE UP!
?
WE'RE DOOMED.
DO YOU THINK THEY'LL MELT US DOWN?
GRNN
DON'T SHOOT! *DON'T SHOOT!*
RABBA RABBA!
WILL THIS NEVER END?
!!
BEE-ROOP! VEEP!

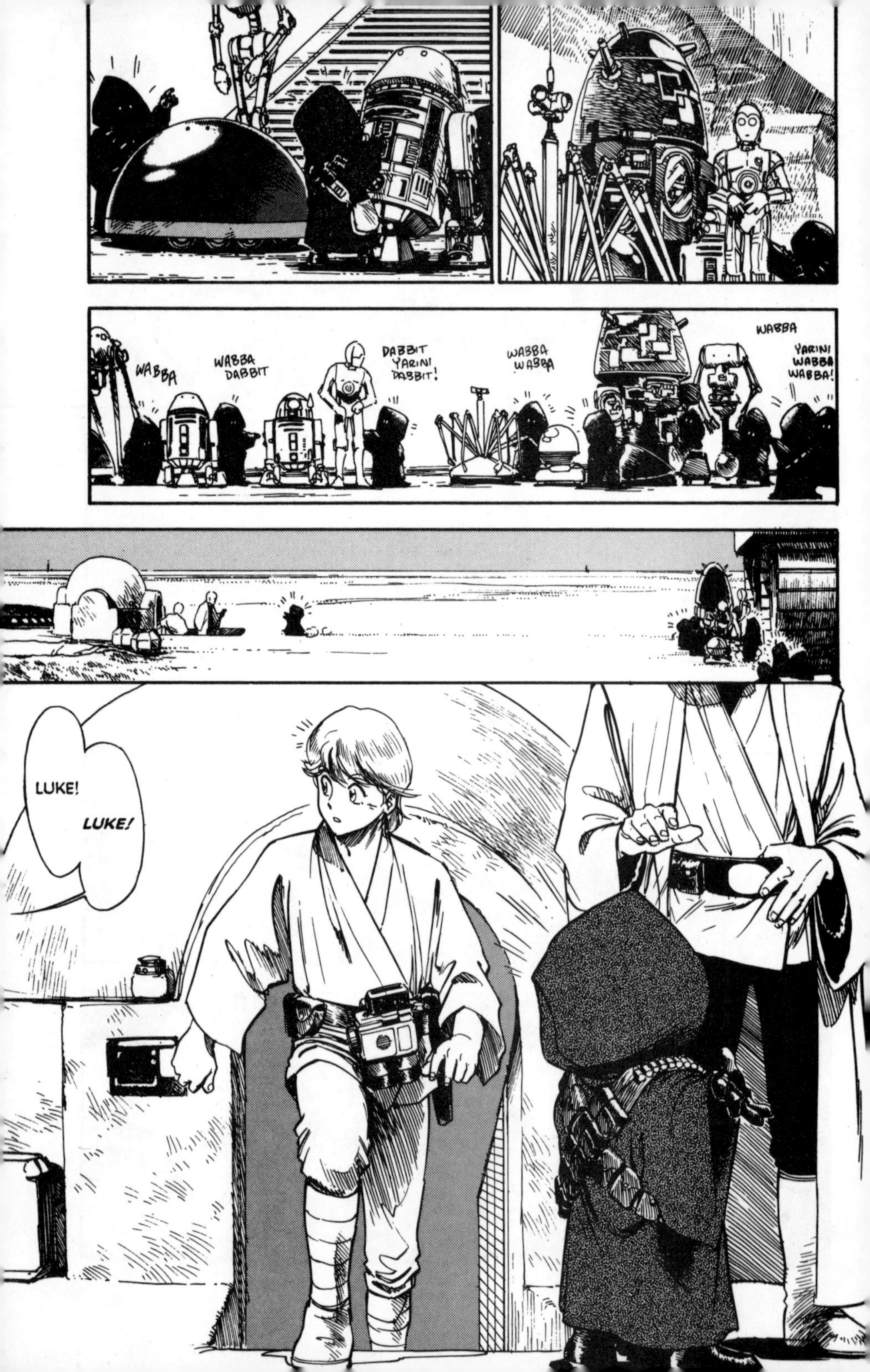
WABBA
WABBA DABBIT
DABBIT YARINI DABBIT!
WABBA WABBA
WABBA
YARINI WABBA WABBA!
LUKE! LUKE!

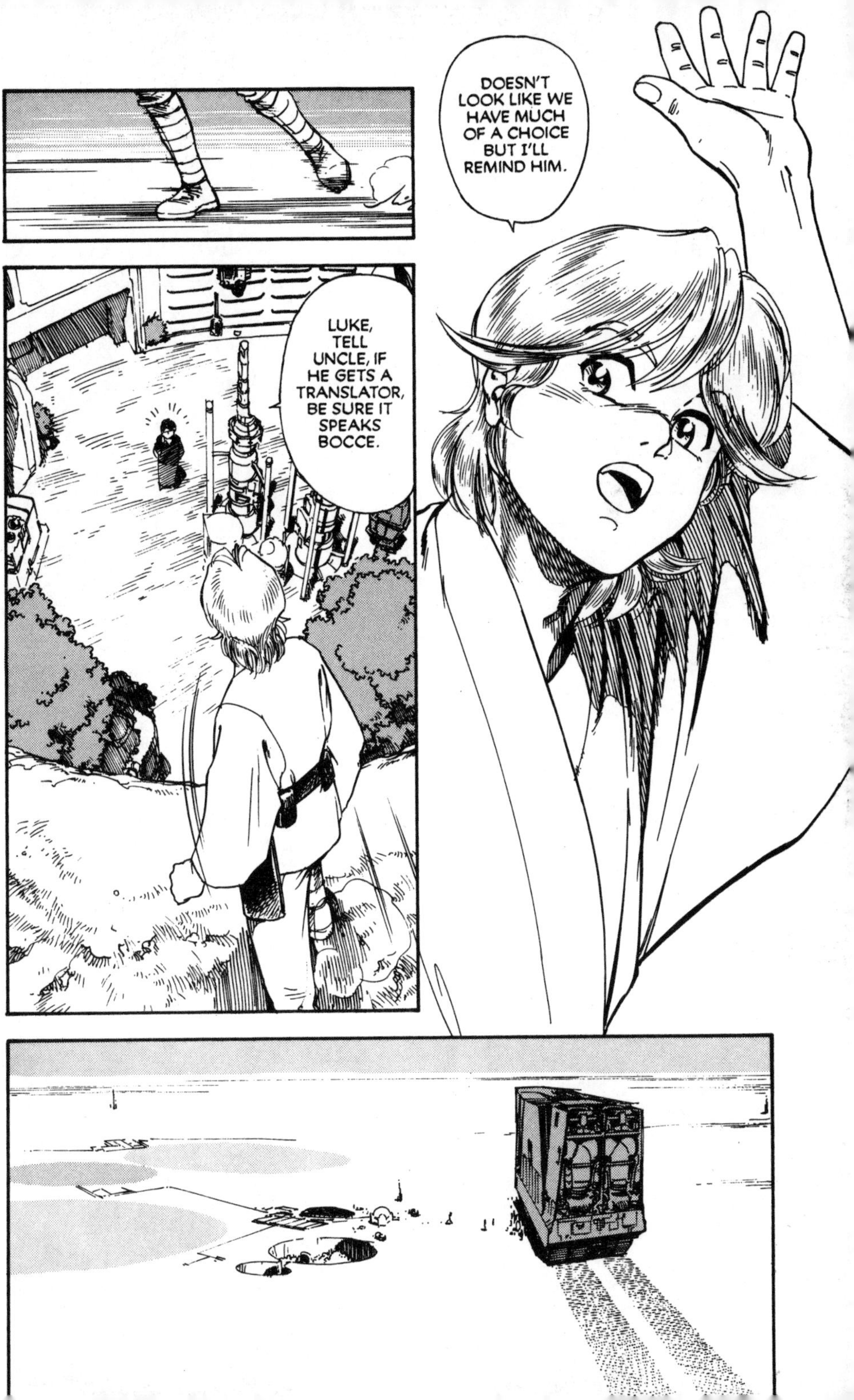
LUKE, TELL UNCLE, IF HE GETS A TRANSLATOR, BE SURE IT SPEAKS BOCCE.
DOESN'T LOOK LIKE WE HAVE MUCH OF A CHOICE BUT I'LL REMIND HIM.

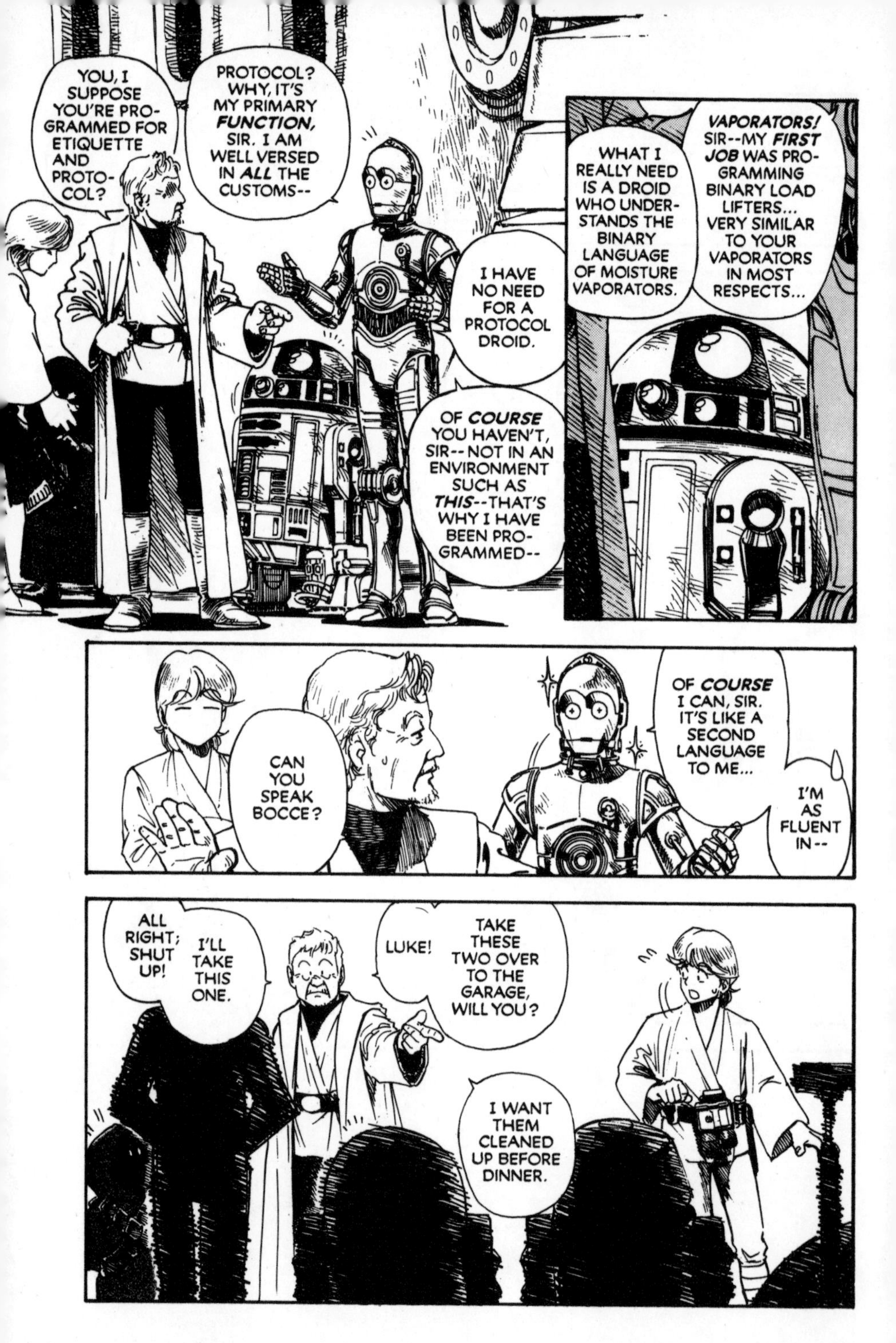
YOU, I SUPPOSE YOU'RE PROGRAMMED FOR ETIQUETTE AND PROTOCOL?
PROTOCOL? WHY, IT'S MY PRIMARY *FUNCTION,* SIR. I AM WELL VERSED IN *ALL* THE CUSTOMS--
I HAVE NO NEED FOR A PROTOCOL DROID.
OF *COURSE* YOU HAVEN'T, SIR--NOT IN AN ENVIRONMENT SUCH AS *THIS*--THAT'S WHY I HAVE BEEN PROGRAMMED--
WHAT I REALLY NEED IS A DROID WHO UNDERSTANDS THE BINARY LANGUAGE OF MOISTURE VAPORATORS.
VAPORATORS! SIR--MY *FIRST JOB* WAS PROGRAMMING BINARY LOAD LIFTERS... VERY SIMILAR TO YOUR VAPORATORS IN MOST RESPECTS...
CAN YOU SPEAK BOCCE?
OF *COURSE* I CAN, SIR. IT'S LIKE A SECOND LANGUAGE TO ME...
I'M AS FLUENT IN--
ALL RIGHT; SHUT UP!
I'LL TAKE THIS ONE.
LUKE!
TAKE THESE TWO OVER TO THE GARAGE, WILL YOU?
I WANT THEM CLEANED UP BEFORE DINNER.

--BUT I WAS GOING INTO TOSCHE STATION--

--TO PICK UP SOME POWER CONVERTERS...

YOU CAN WASTE TIME WITH YOUR FRIENDS WHEN YOUR CHORES ARE DONE. NOW, COME ON, GET TO IT!

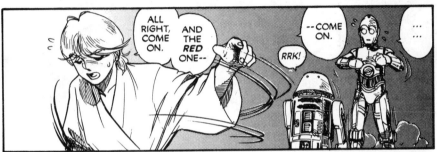

ALL RIGHT, COME ON.

AND THE *RED* ONE--

RRK!

--COME ON.

...

...

BEE-OOP!

KLKLK

WAB?

DABBIT!

REE...

RRK...

OOP OOP...

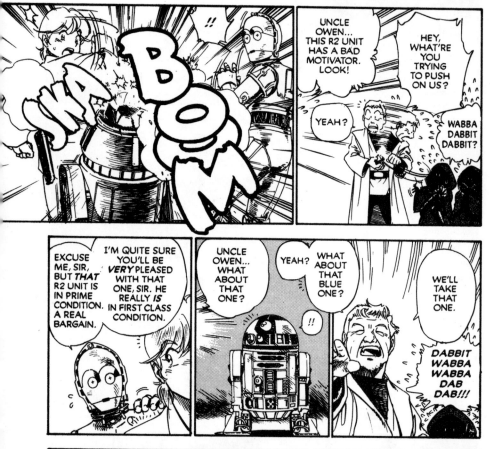

SKA BOOM

!!

UNCLE OWEN... THIS R2 UNIT HAS A BAD MOTIVATOR. LOOK!

HEY, WHAT'RE YOU TRYING TO PUSH ON US?

YEAH?

WABBA DABBIT DABBIT?

EXCUSE ME, SIR, BUT *THAT* R2 UNIT IS IN PRIME CONDITION. A REAL BARGAIN.

I'M QUITE SURE YOU'LL BE *VERY* PLEASED WITH THAT ONE, SIR. HE REALLY *IS* IN FIRST CLASS CONDITION.

UNCLE OWEN... WHAT ABOUT THAT ONE?

YEAH?

WHAT ABOUT THAT BLUE ONE?

WE'LL TAKE THAT ONE.

!!

DABBIT WABBA WABBA DAB DAB!!!

NOW, DON'T YOU FORGET THIS!

REEP! BOOP!

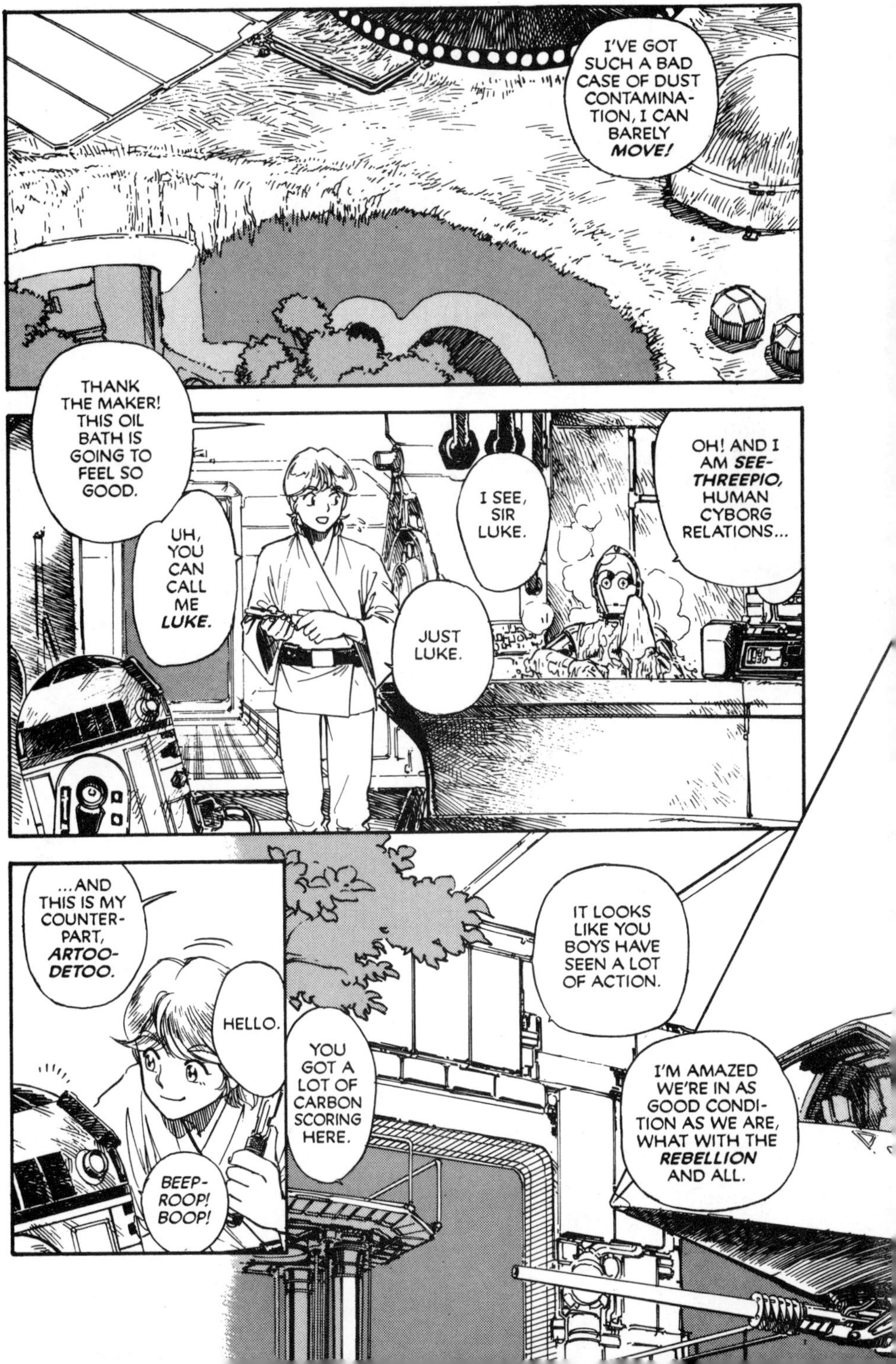
I'VE GOT SUCH A BAD CASE OF DUST CONTAMINA-TION, I CAN BARELY ***MOVE!***
THANK THE MAKER! THIS OIL BATH IS GOING TO FEEL SO GOOD.
UH, YOU CAN CALL ME ***LUKE.***
I SEE, SIR LUKE.
JUST LUKE.
OH! AND I AM ***SEE-THREEPIO,*** HUMAN CYBORG RELATIONS...
...AND THIS IS MY COUNTER-PART, ***ARTOO-DETOO.***
HELLO.
BEEP-ROOP! BOOP!
YOU GOT A LOT OF CARBON SCORING HERE.
IT LOOKS LIKE YOU BOYS HAVE SEEN A LOT OF ACTION.
I'M AMAZED WE'RE IN AS GOOD CONDI-TION AS WE ARE, WHAT WITH THE ***REBELLION*** AND ALL.

YOU KNOW OF THE REBELLION AGAINST THE EMPIRE?

THAT'S HOW WE CAME TO BE IN YOUR SERVICE.

THERE'S NOT MUCH TO TELL. I'M NOT MUCH MORE THAN AN INTERPRETER, AND NOT VERY GOOD AT TELLING STORIES.

IT JUST ISN'T FAIR.

IS THERE ANY- THING I MIGHT DO TO HELP?

WELL, NOT UNLESS YOU CAN ALTER TIME, SPEED UP THE HARVEST, OR TELEPORT ME *OFF* THIS ROCK!

I DON'T THINK SO, SIR.

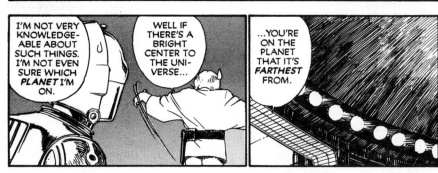

I'M NOT VERY KNOWLEDGE- ABLE ABOUT SUCH THINGS. I'M NOT EVEN SURE WHICH *PLANET* I'M ON.

WELL IF THERE'S A BRIGHT CENTER TO THE UNI- VERSE...

...YOU'RE ON THE PLANET THAT IT'S *FARTHEST* FROM.

"LUKE, I DIDN'T COME BACK JUST TO SAY GOOD- BYE...

"I SHOULDN'T TELL YOU THIS, BUT YOU'RE THE ONLY ONE I CAN TRUST... AND IF I DON'T COME BACK, I WANT SOMEBODY TO KNOW.

"I MADE SOME FRIENDS AT THE ACADEMY. WHEN OUR FRIGATE GOES TO ONE OF THE CENTRAL SYSTEMS, WE'RE GOING TO JUMP SHIP AND JOIN THE *ALLIANCE...*"

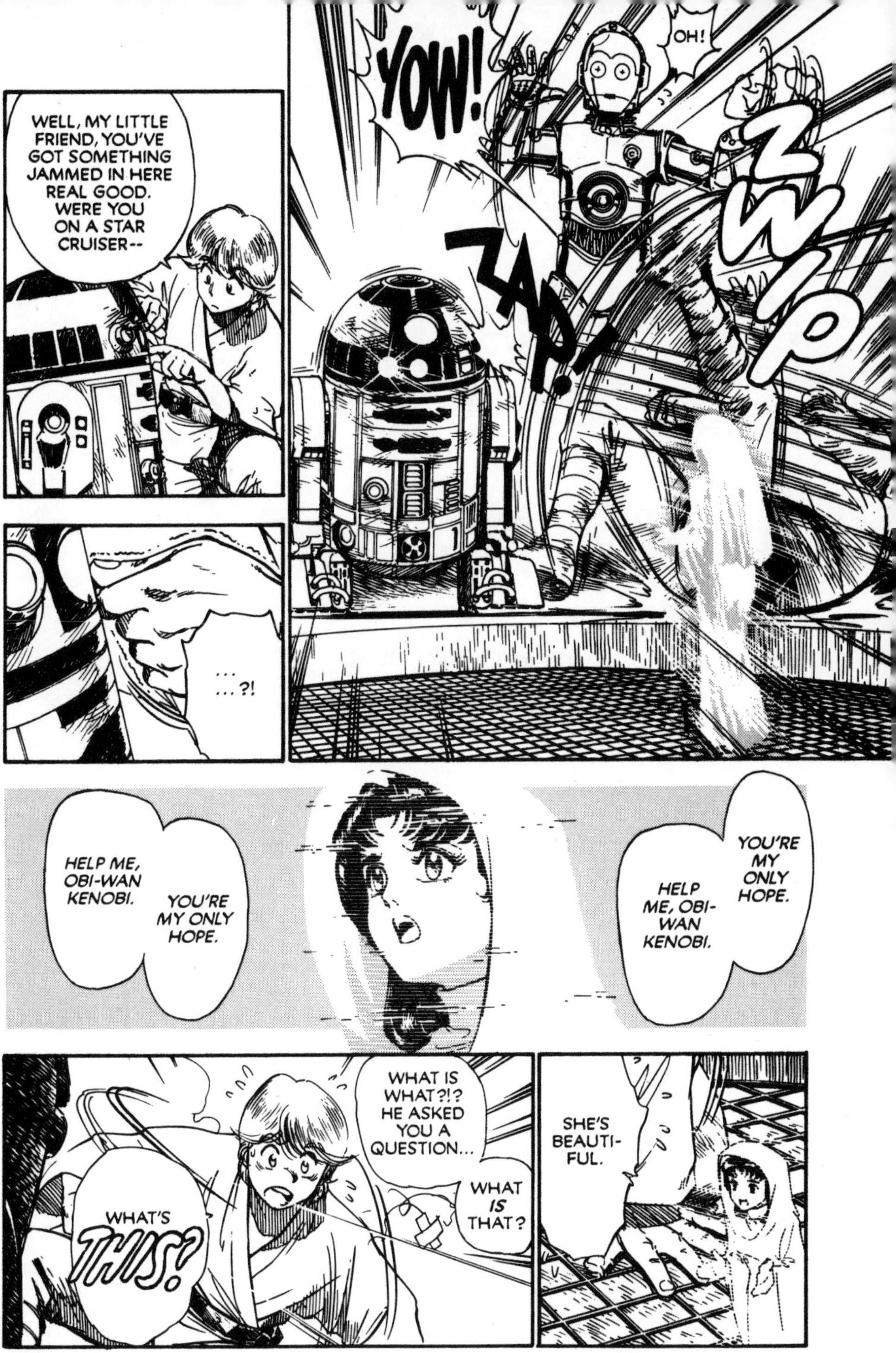
WELL, MY LITTLE FRIEND, YOU'VE GOT SOMETHING JAMMED IN HERE REAL GOOD. WERE YOU ON A STAR CRUISER--
...
...?!
YOW!
OH!
ZAP!
ZWIP
HELP ME, OBI-WAN KENOBI.
YOU'RE MY ONLY HOPE.
HELP ME, OBI-WAN KENOBI.
YOU'RE MY ONLY HOPE.
WHAT'S THIS?
WHAT IS WHAT?!? HE ASKED YOU A QUESTION...
WHAT IS THAT?
SHE'S BEAUTI-FUL.

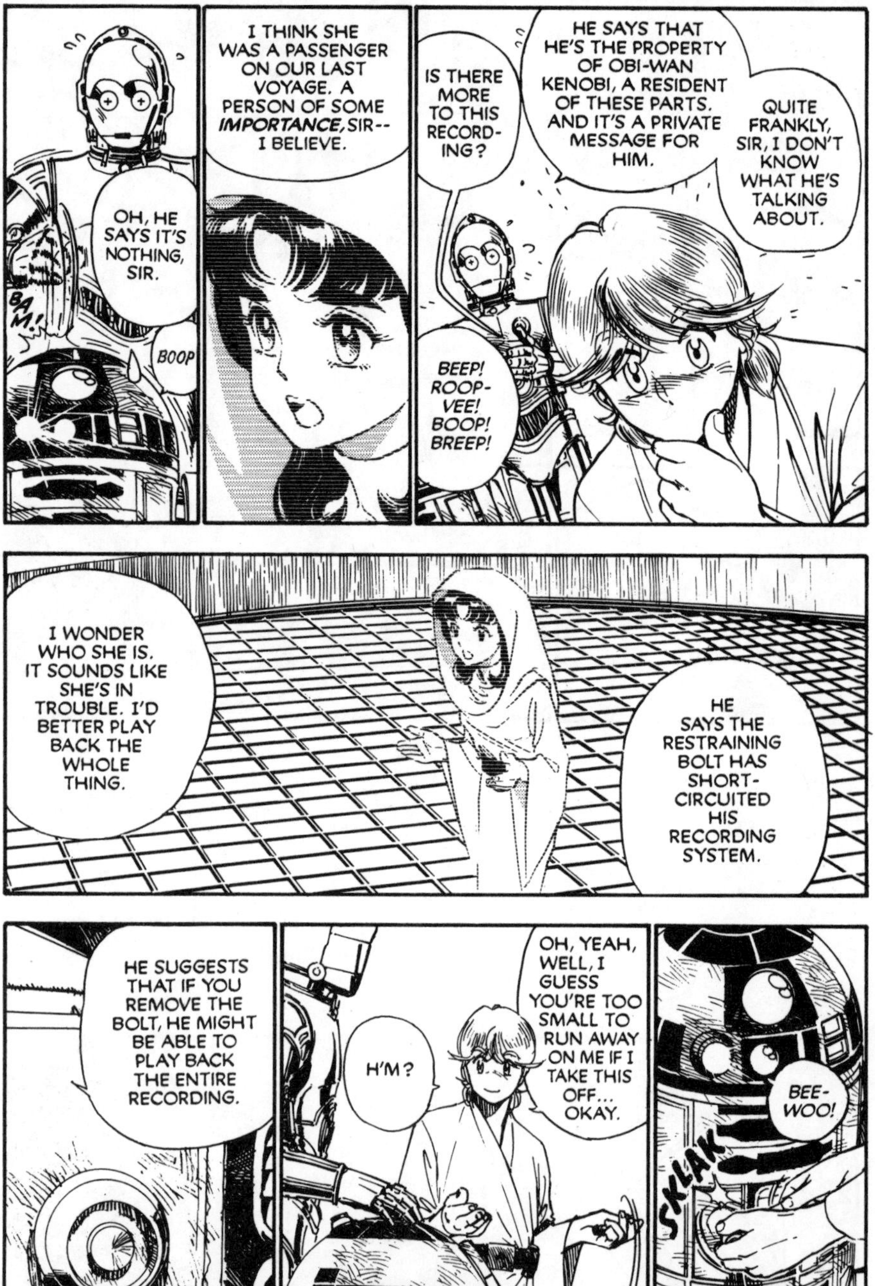
OH, HE SAYS IT'S NOTHING, SIR.
BAM!
BOOP
I THINK SHE WAS A PASSENGER ON OUR LAST VOYAGE. A PERSON OF SOME *IMPORTANCE,* SIR-- I BELIEVE.
IS THERE MORE TO THIS RECORD-ING?
HE SAYS THAT HE'S THE PROPERTY OF OBI-WAN KENOBI, A RESIDENT OF THESE PARTS. AND IT'S A PRIVATE MESSAGE FOR HIM.
QUITE FRANKLY, SIR, I DON'T KNOW WHAT HE'S TALKING ABOUT.
BEEP! ROOP-VEE! BOOP! BREEP!
I WONDER WHO SHE IS. IT SOUNDS LIKE SHE'S IN TROUBLE. I'D BETTER PLAY BACK THE WHOLE THING.
HE SAYS THE RESTRAINING BOLT HAS SHORT-CIRCUITED HIS RECORDING SYSTEM.
HE SUGGESTS THAT IF YOU REMOVE THE BOLT, HE MIGHT BE ABLE TO PLAY BACK THE ENTIRE RECORDING.
H'M?
OH, YEAH, WELL, I GUESS YOU'RE TOO SMALL TO RUN AWAY ON ME IF I TAKE THIS OFF... OKAY.
BEE-WOO!
SKLAK

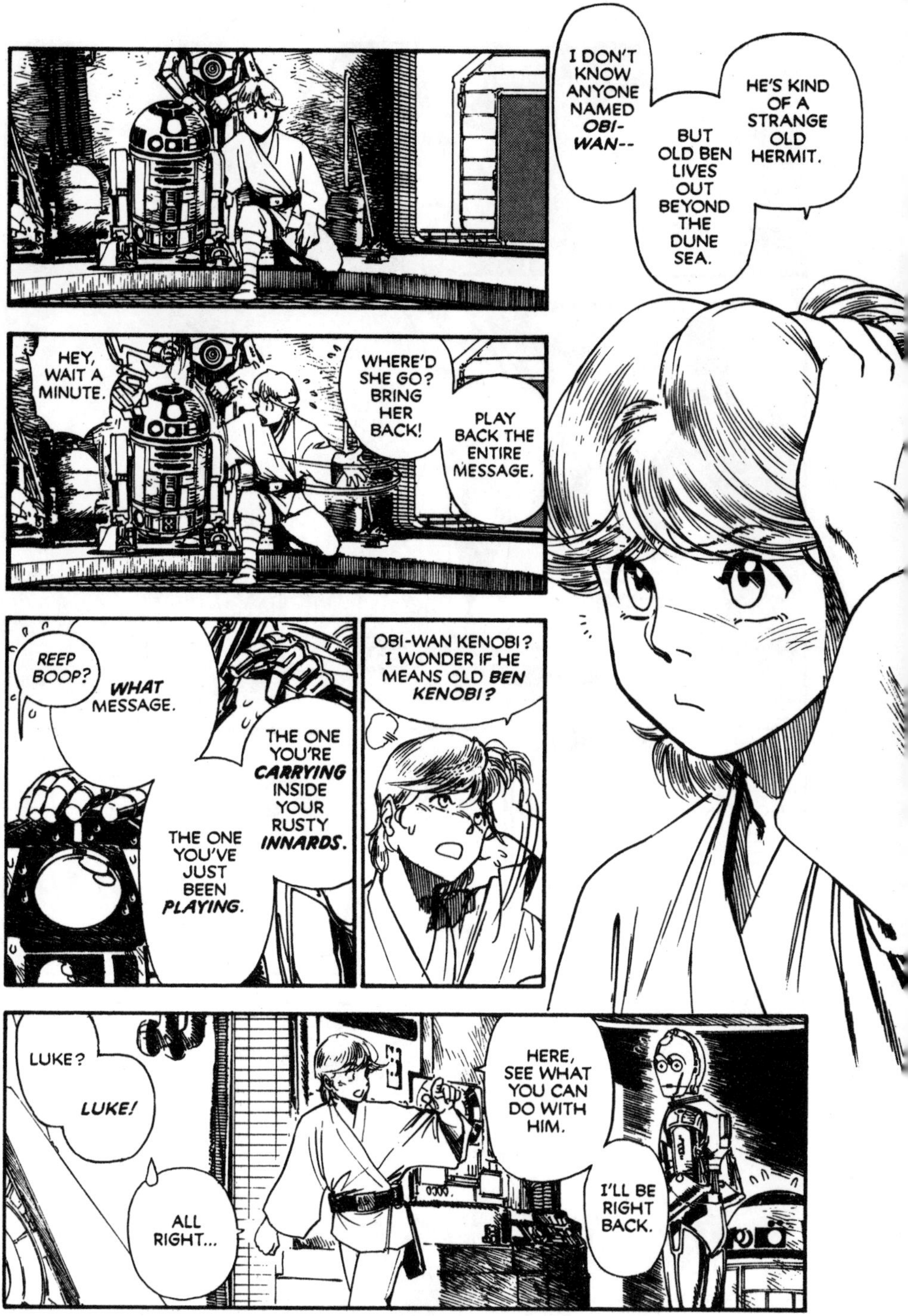

HEY, WAIT A MINUTE.
WHERE'D SHE GO? BRING HER BACK!
PLAY BACK THE ENTIRE MESSAGE.
REEP BOOP?
WHAT MESSAGE.
THE ONE YOU'RE CARRYING INSIDE YOUR RUSTY INNARDS.
THE ONE YOU'VE JUST BEEN PLAYING.
OBI-WAN KENOBI? I WONDER IF HE MEANS OLD BEN KENOBI?
I DON'T KNOW ANYONE NAMED OBI-WAN--
BUT OLD BEN LIVES OUT BEYOND THE DUNE SEA.
HE'S KIND OF A STRANGE OLD HERMIT.
LUKE?
LUKE!
ALL RIGHT...
HERE, SEE WHAT YOU CAN DO WITH HIM.
I'LL BE RIGHT BACK.

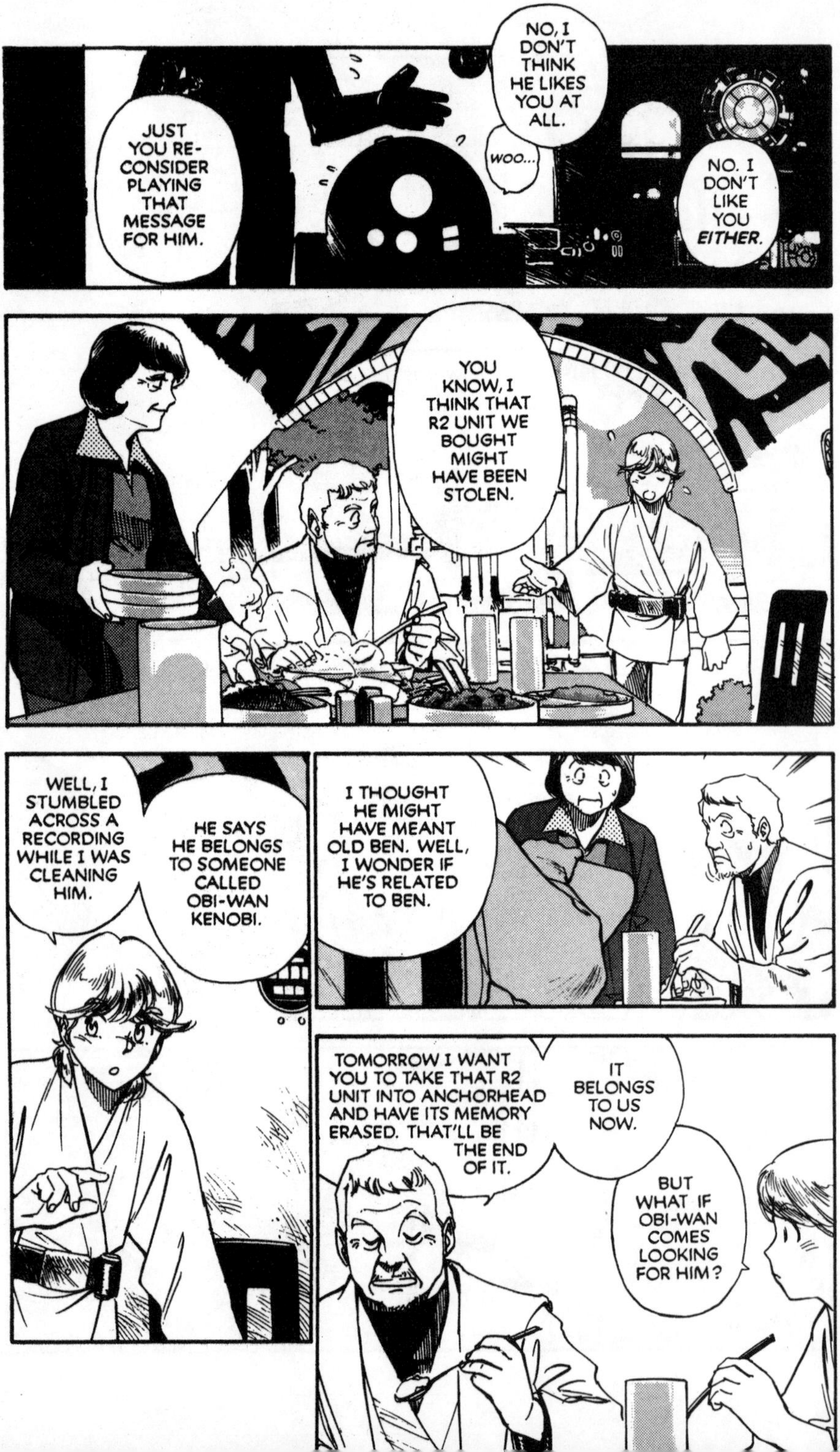
JUST YOU RE-CONSIDER PLAYING THAT MESSAGE FOR HIM.
NO, I DON'T THINK HE LIKES YOU AT ALL.
WOO...
NO. I DON'T LIKE YOU *EITHER*.
YOU KNOW, I THINK THAT R2 UNIT WE BOUGHT MIGHT HAVE BEEN STOLEN.
WELL, I STUMBLED ACROSS A RECORDING WHILE I WAS CLEANING HIM.
HE SAYS HE BELONGS TO SOMEONE CALLED OBI-WAN KENOBI.
I THOUGHT HE MIGHT HAVE MEANT OLD BEN. WELL, I WONDER IF HE'S RELATED TO BEN.
TOMORROW I WANT YOU TO TAKE THAT R2 UNIT INTO ANCHORHEAD AND HAVE ITS MEMORY ERASED. THAT'LL BE THE END OF IT.
IT BELONGS TO US NOW.
BUT WHAT IF OBI-WAN COMES LOOKING FOR HIM?

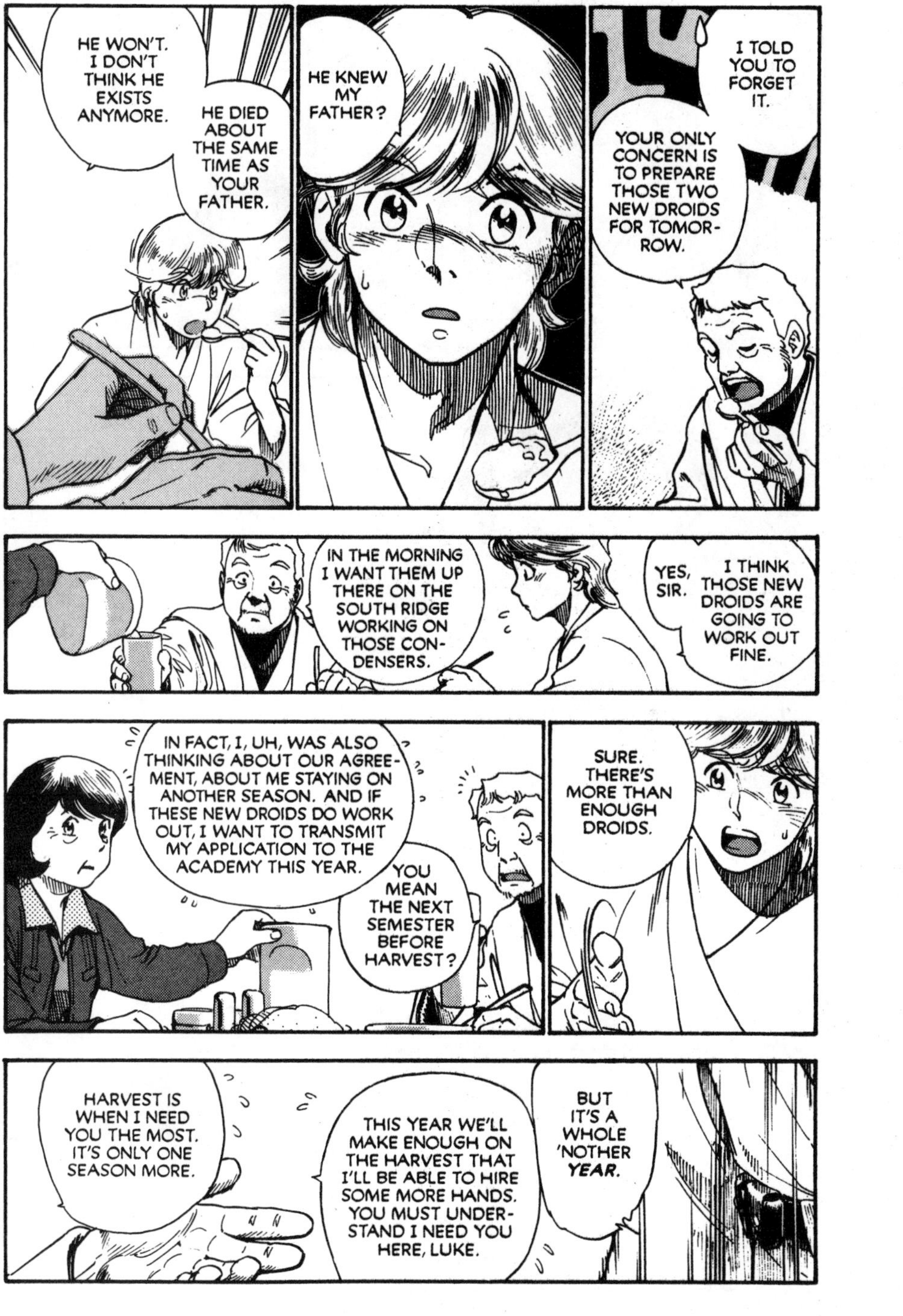
HE WON'T. I DON'T THINK HE EXISTS ANYMORE.
HE DIED ABOUT THE SAME TIME AS YOUR FATHER.
HE KNEW MY FATHER?
I TOLD YOU TO FORGET IT.
YOUR ONLY CONCERN IS TO PREPARE THOSE TWO NEW DROIDS FOR TOMOR-ROW.
IN THE MORNING I WANT THEM UP THERE ON THE SOUTH RIDGE WORKING ON THOSE CON-DENSERS.
YES, SIR.
I THINK THOSE NEW DROIDS ARE GOING TO WORK OUT FINE.
IN FACT, I, UH, WAS ALSO THINKING ABOUT OUR AGREE-MENT, ABOUT ME STAYING ON ANOTHER SEASON. AND IF THESE NEW DROIDS DO WORK OUT, I WANT TO TRANSMIT MY APPLICATION TO THE ACADEMY THIS YEAR.
YOU MEAN THE NEXT SEMESTER BEFORE HARVEST?
SURE. THERE'S MORE THAN ENOUGH DROIDS.
HARVEST IS WHEN I NEED YOU THE MOST. IT'S ONLY ONE SEASON MORE.
THIS YEAR WE'LL MAKE ENOUGH ON THE HARVEST THAT I'LL BE ABLE TO HIRE SOME MORE HANDS. YOU MUST UNDER-STAND I NEED YOU HERE, LUKE.
BUT IT'S A WHOLE 'NOTHER *YEAR.*

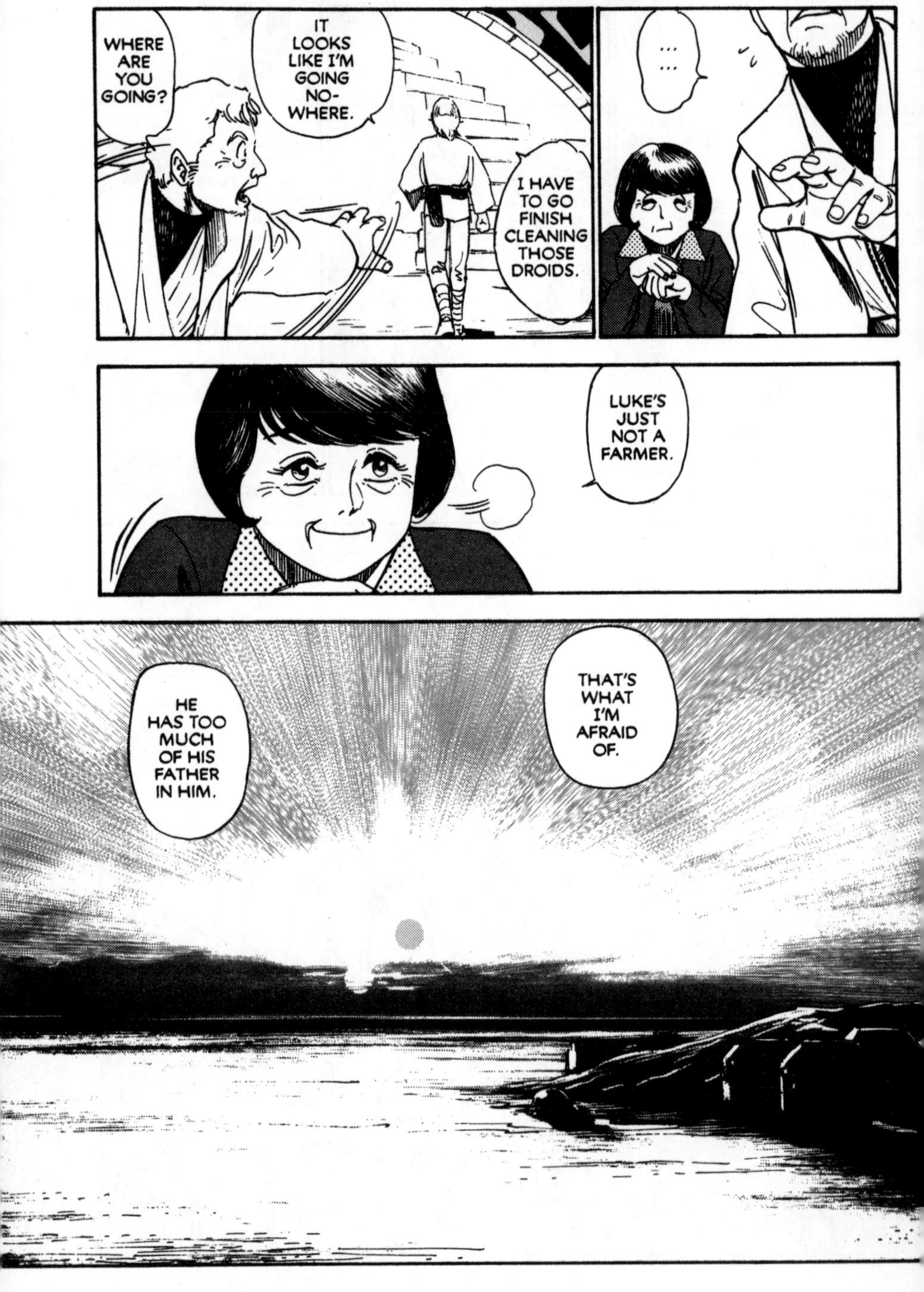
WHERE ARE YOU GOING?
IT LOOKS LIKE I'M GOING NO-WHERE.
I HAVE TO GO FINISH CLEANING THOSE DROIDS.
...
...
LUKE'S JUST NOT A FARMER.
HE HAS TOO MUCH OF HIS FATHER IN HIM.
THAT'S WHAT I'M AFRAID OF.

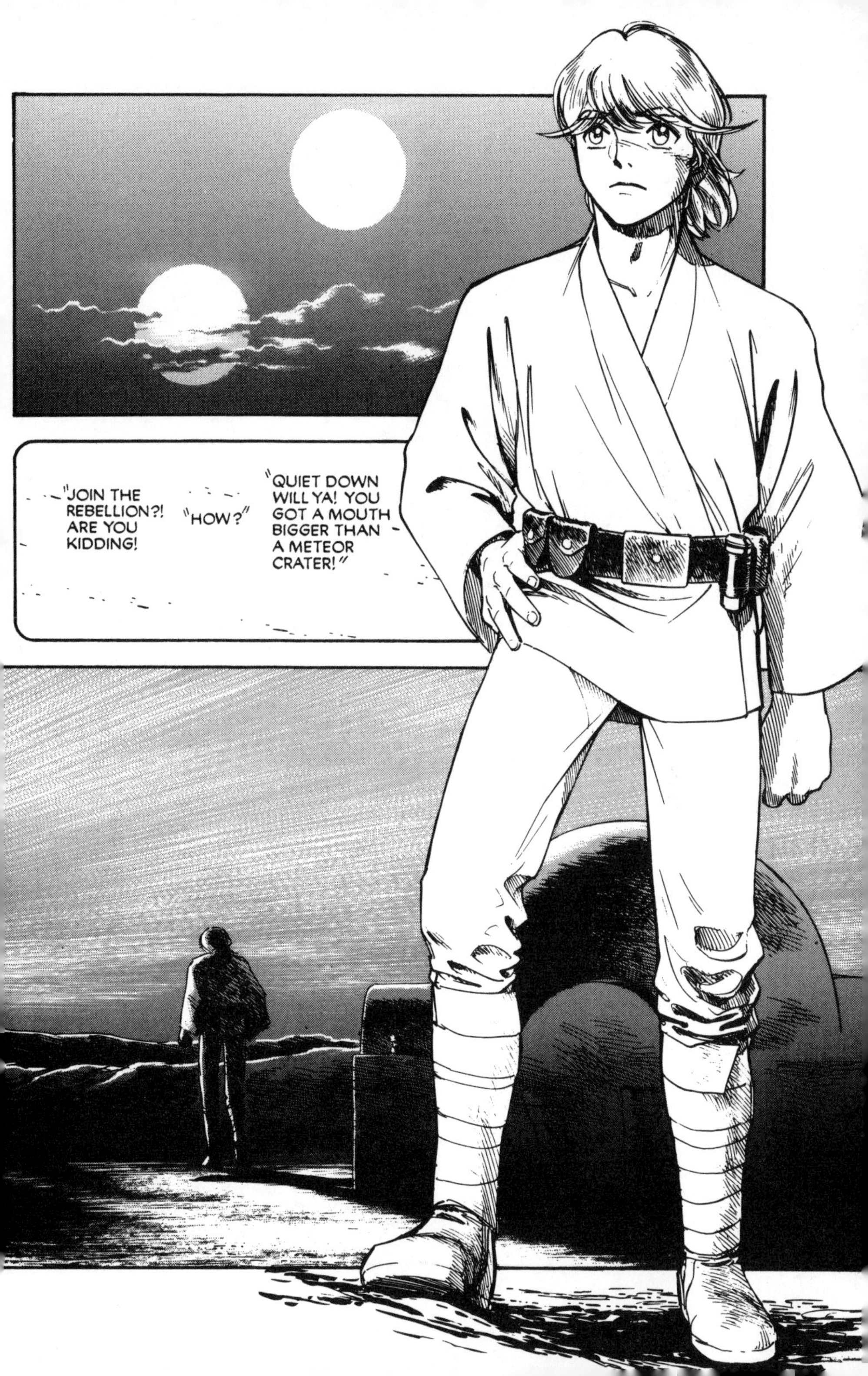
"JOIN THE REBELLION?! ARE YOU KIDDING!
"HOW?"
"QUIET DOWN WILL YA! YOU GOT A MOUTH BIGGER THAN A METEOR CRATER!"

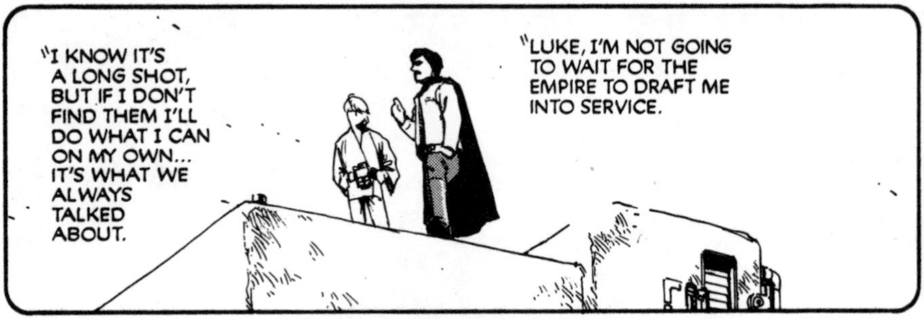
"I KNOW IT'S A LONG SHOT, BUT IF I DON'T FIND THEM I'LL DO WHAT I CAN ON MY OWN... IT'S WHAT WE ALWAYS TALKED ABOUT.
"LUKE, I'M NOT GOING TO WAIT FOR THE EMPIRE TO DRAFT ME INTO SERVICE.

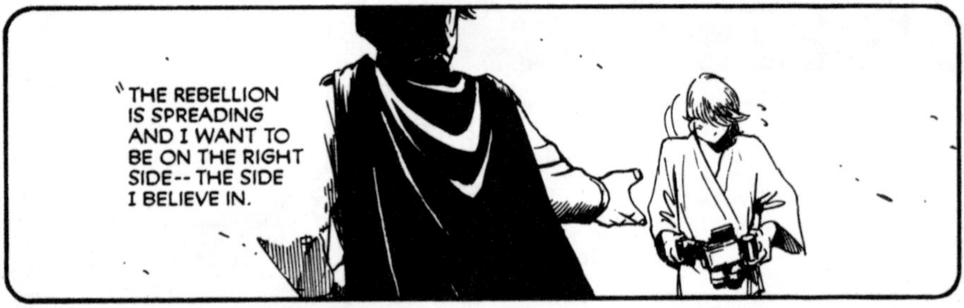
"THE REBELLION IS SPREADING AND I WANT TO BE ON THE RIGHT SIDE-- THE SIDE I BELIEVE IN.

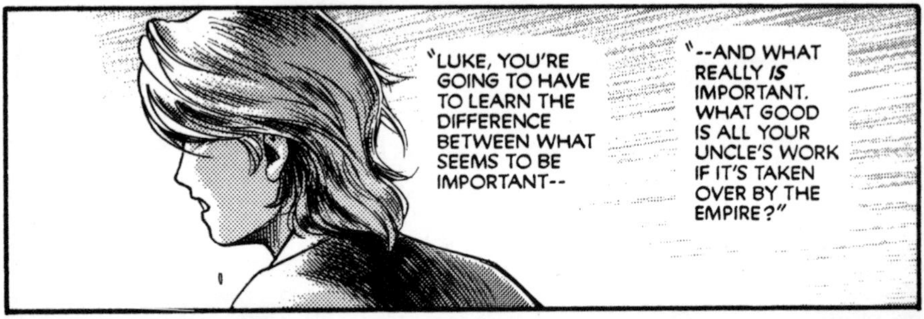
"LUKE, YOU'RE GOING TO HAVE TO LEARN THE DIFFERENCE BETWEEN WHAT SEEMS TO BE IMPORTANT--
"--AND WHAT REALLY *IS* IMPORTANT. WHAT GOOD IS ALL YOUR UNCLE'S WORK IF IT'S TAKEN OVER BY THE EMPIRE?"

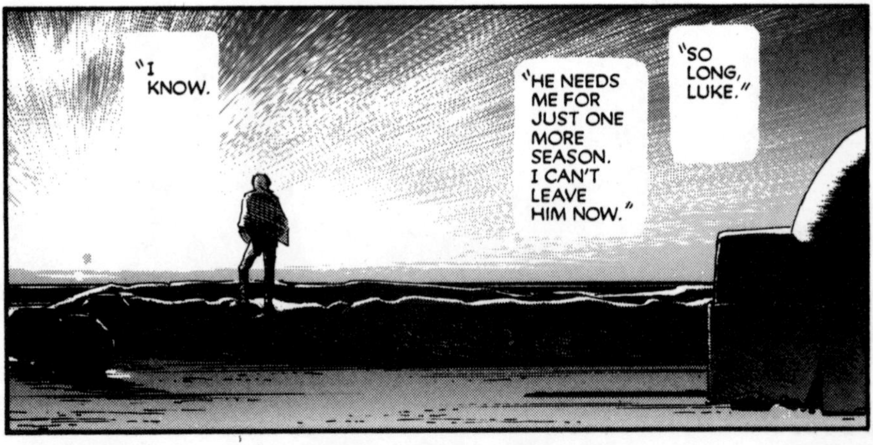
"I KNOW.
"HE NEEDS ME FOR JUST ONE MORE SEASON. I CAN'T LEAVE HIM NOW."
"SO LONG, LUKE."

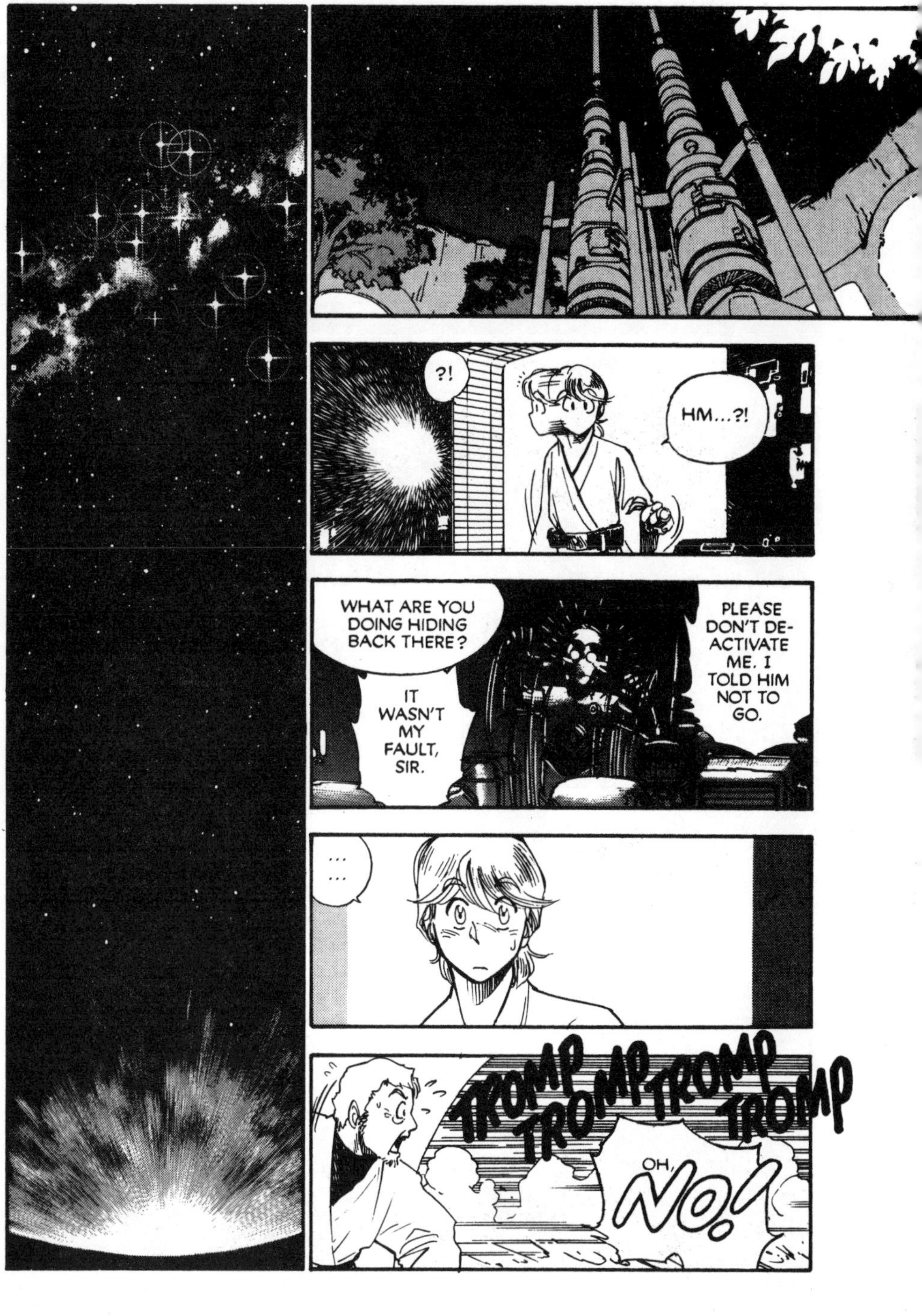
?!
HM...?!
WHAT ARE YOU DOING HIDING BACK THERE?
IT WASN'T MY FAULT, SIR.
PLEASE DON'T DE-ACTIVATE ME. I TOLD HIM NOT TO GO.
...
...
TROMP TROMP TROMP TROMP
OH, NO!

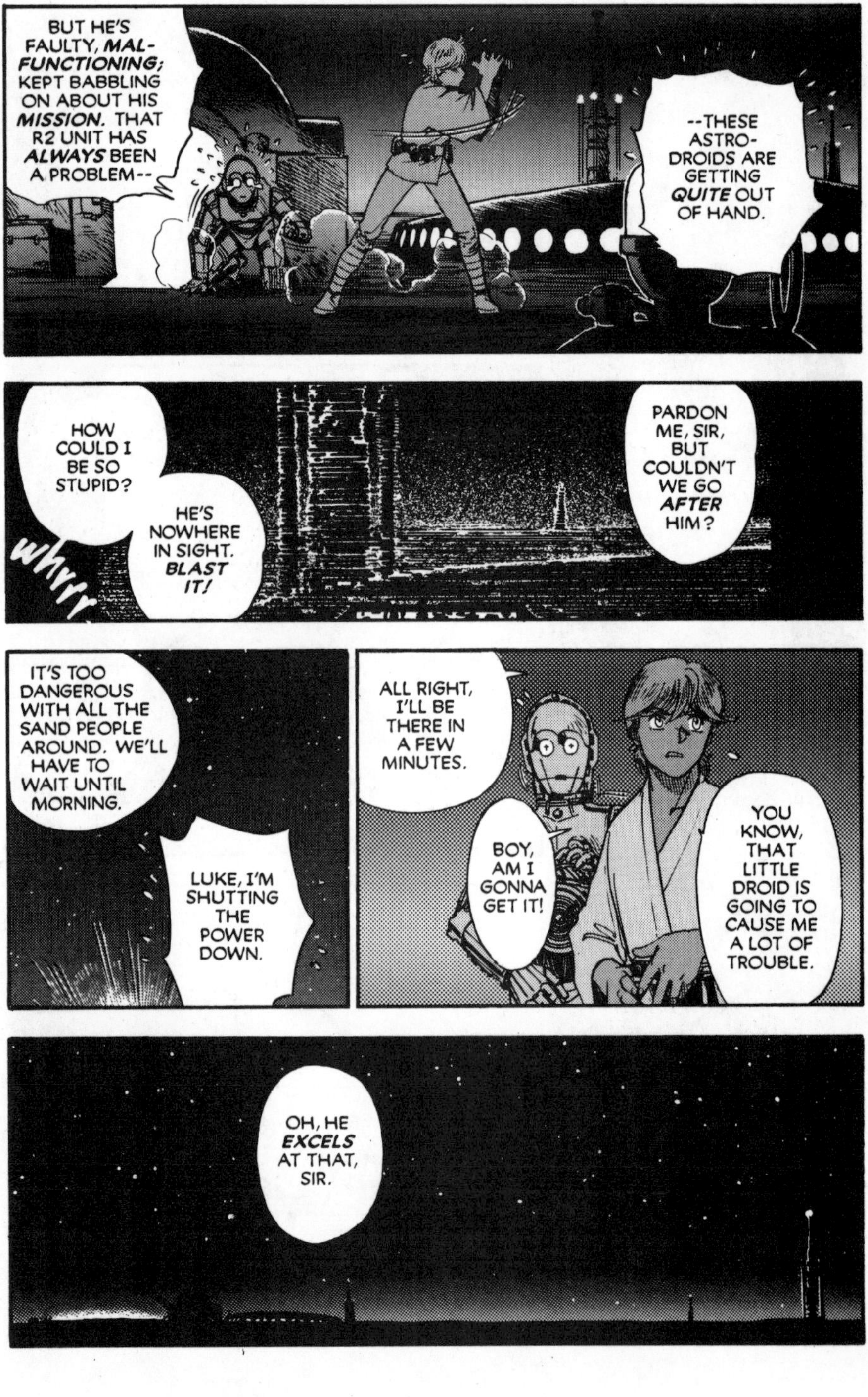
BUT HE'S FAULTY, MAL-FUNCTIONING; KEPT BABBLING ON ABOUT HIS MISSION. THAT R2 UNIT HAS ALWAYS BEEN A PROBLEM--
--THESE ASTRO-DROIDS ARE GETTING QUITE OUT OF HAND.
HOW COULD I BE SO STUPID?
HE'S NOWHERE IN SIGHT. BLAST IT!
whrrr
PARDON ME, SIR, BUT COULDN'T WE GO AFTER HIM?
IT'S TOO DANGEROUS WITH ALL THE SAND PEOPLE AROUND. WE'LL HAVE TO WAIT UNTIL MORNING.
LUKE, I'M SHUTTING THE POWER DOWN.
ALL RIGHT, I'LL BE THERE IN A FEW MINUTES.
BOY, AM I GONNA GET IT!
YOU KNOW, THAT LITTLE DROID IS GOING TO CAUSE ME A LOT OF TROUBLE.
OH, HE EXCELS AT THAT, SIR.

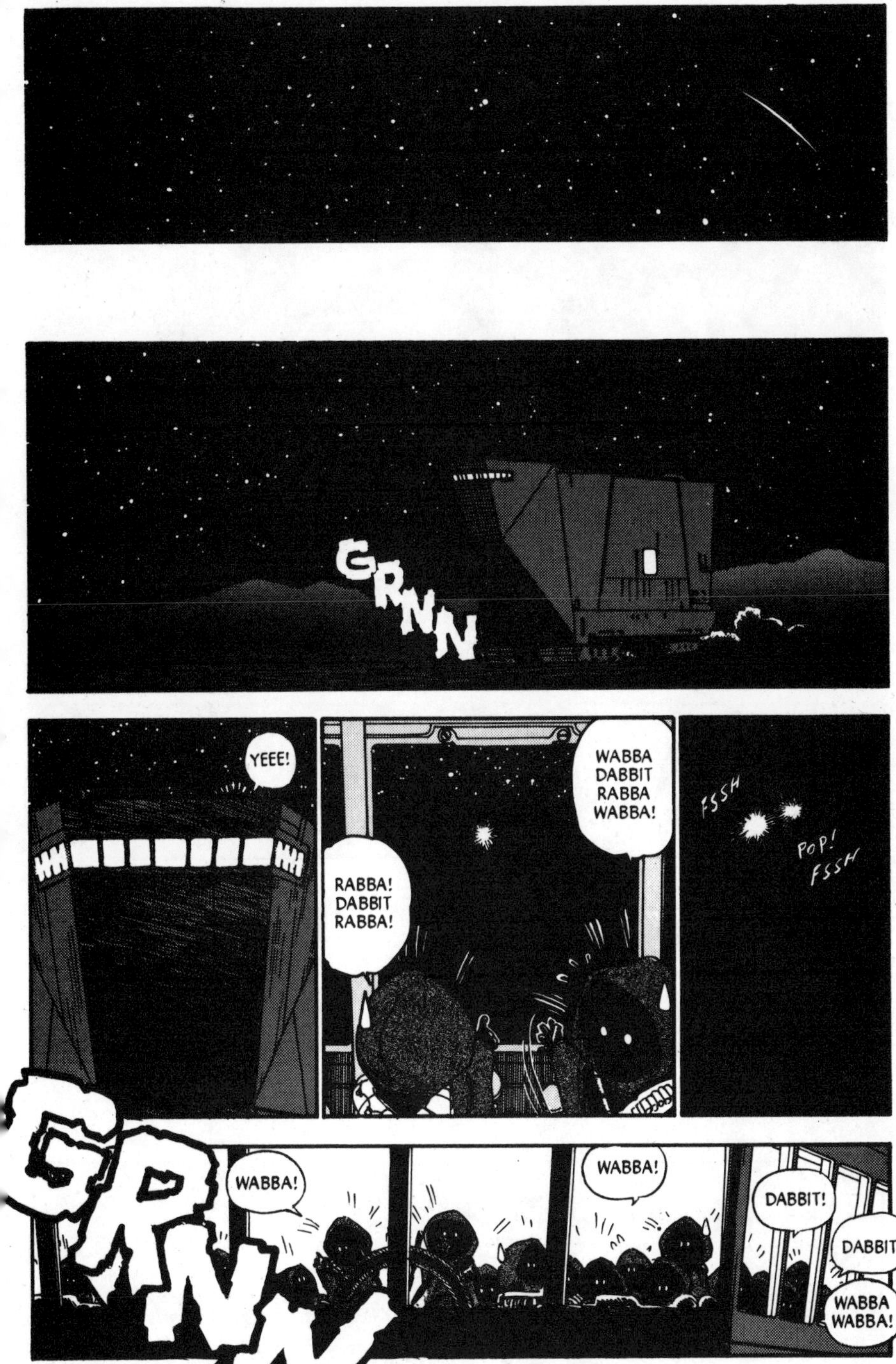
GRNN
YEEE!
WABBA DABBIT RABBA WABBA!
RABBA! DABBIT RABBA!
FSSH
POP! FSSH
GRNN
WABBA!
WABBA!
DABBIT!
DABBIT!
WABBA WABBA!

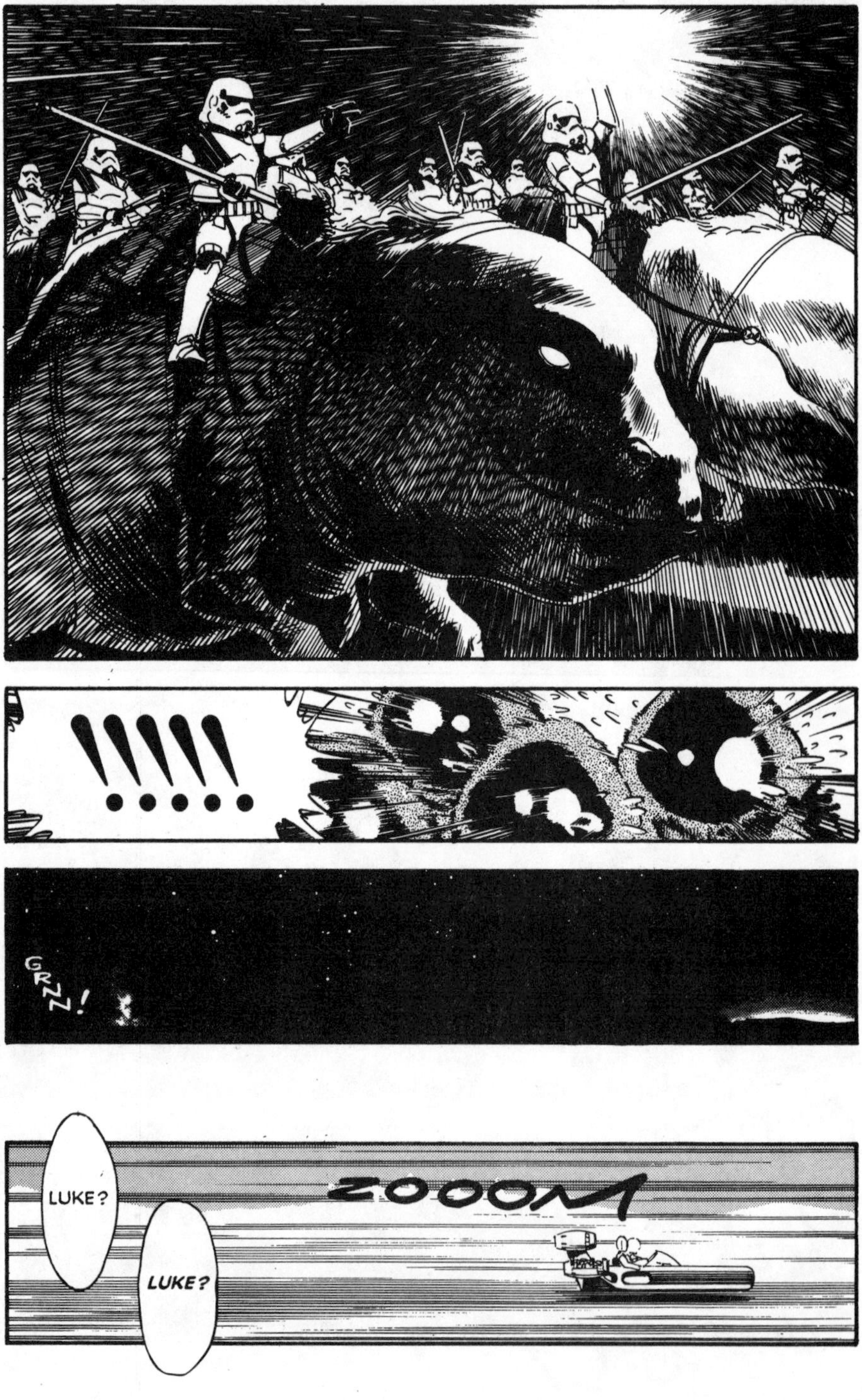
!!!!!
GRNN!
LUKE?
ZOOOM
LUKE?

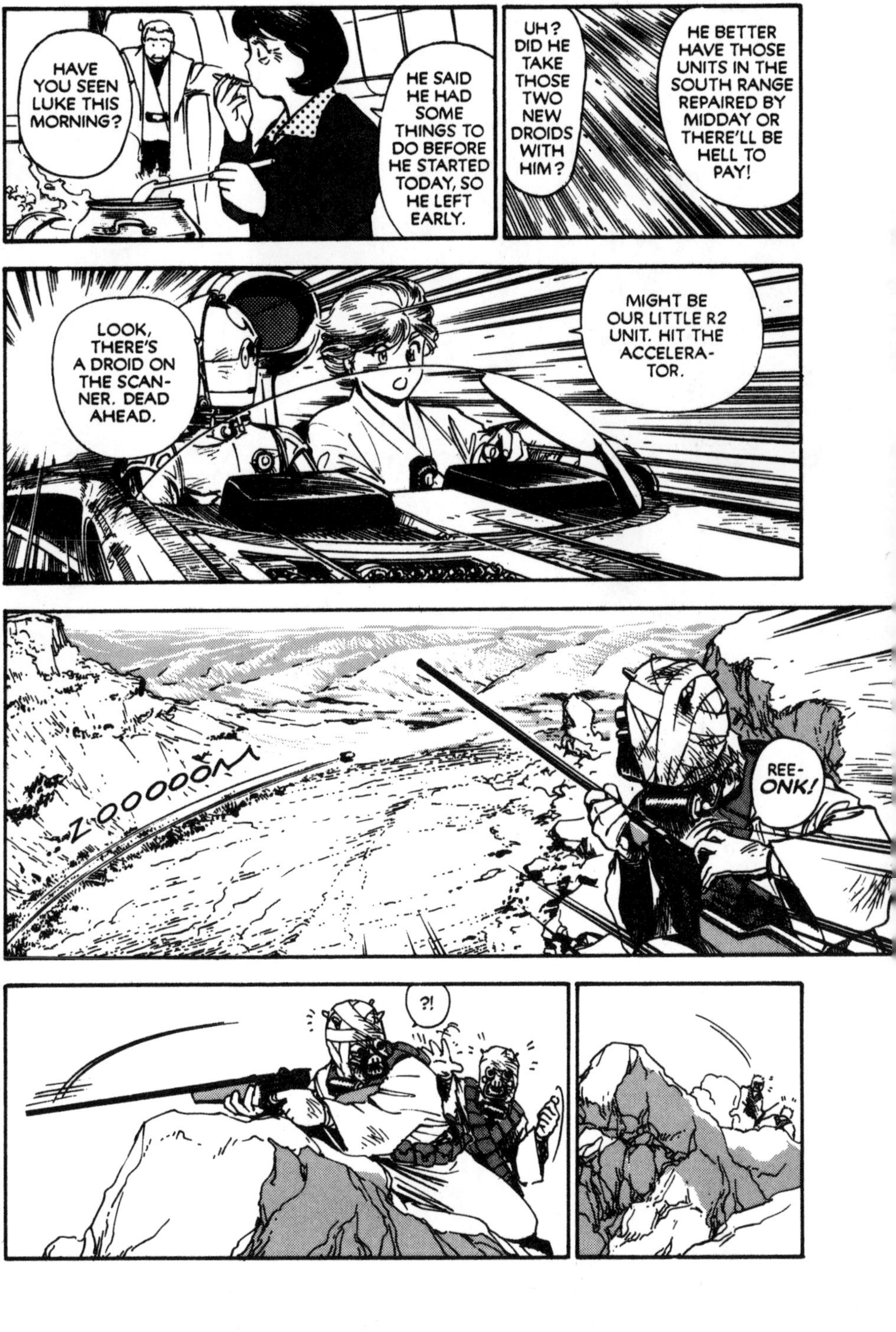
HAVE YOU SEEN LUKE THIS MORNING?
HE SAID HE HAD SOME THINGS TO DO BEFORE HE STARTED TODAY, SO HE LEFT EARLY.
UH? DID HE TAKE THOSE TWO NEW DROIDS WITH HIM?
HE BETTER HAVE THOSE UNITS IN THE SOUTH RANGE REPAIRED BY MIDDAY OR THERE'LL BE HELL TO PAY!
LOOK, THERE'S A DROID ON THE SCANNER. DEAD AHEAD.
MIGHT BE OUR LITTLE R2 UNIT. HIT THE ACCELERATOR.
ZOOOOOOM
REE-ONK!
?!

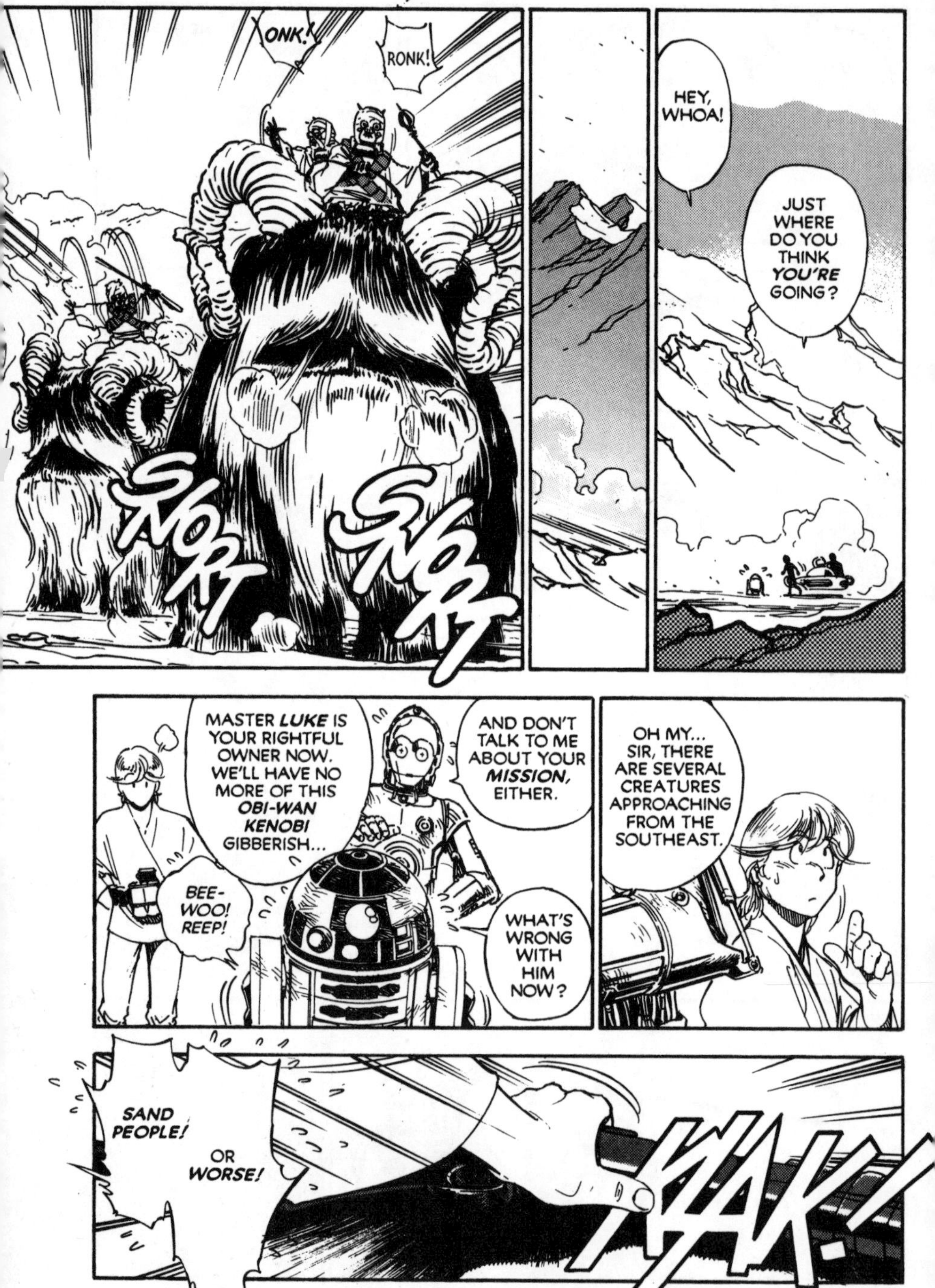
ONK!
RONK!
SNORT
SNORT
HEY, WHOA!
JUST WHERE DO YOU THINK *YOU'RE* GOING?
MASTER *LUKE* IS YOUR RIGHTFUL OWNER NOW. WE'LL HAVE NO MORE OF THIS *OBI-WAN KENOBI* GIBBERISH...
BEE-WOO! REEP!
AND DON'T TALK TO ME ABOUT YOUR *MISSION,* EITHER.
WHAT'S WRONG WITH HIM NOW?
OH MY... SIR, THERE ARE SEVERAL CREATURES APPROACHING FROM THE SOUTHEAST.
SAND PEOPLE!
OR *WORSE!*
YAK!

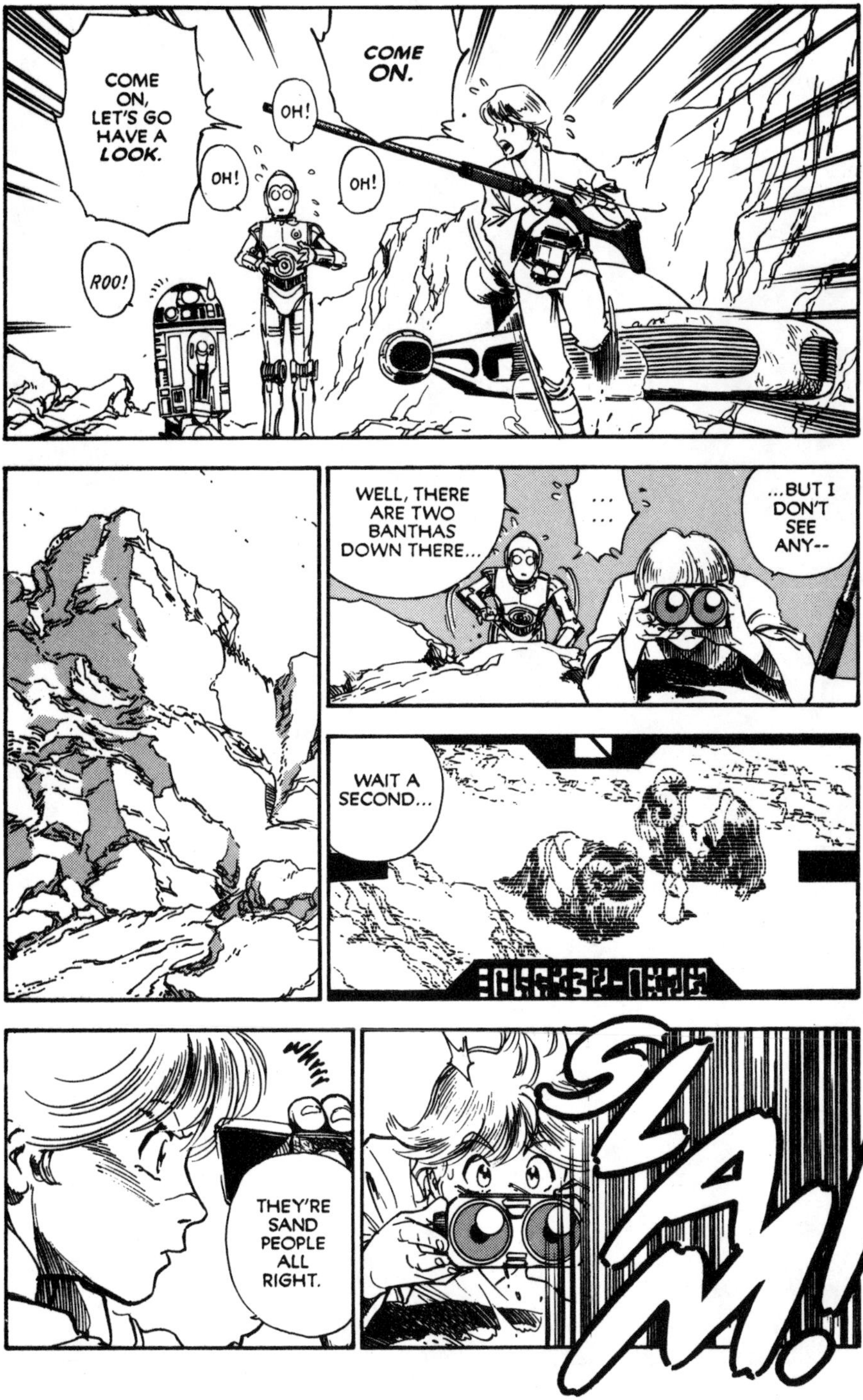
COME ON, LET'S GO HAVE A *LOOK.*
OH!
OH!
OH!
COME ON.
ROO!
WELL, THERE ARE TWO BANTHAS DOWN THERE...
... ...
...BUT I DON'T SEE ANY--
WAIT A SECOND...
THEY'RE SAND PEOPLE ALL RIGHT.

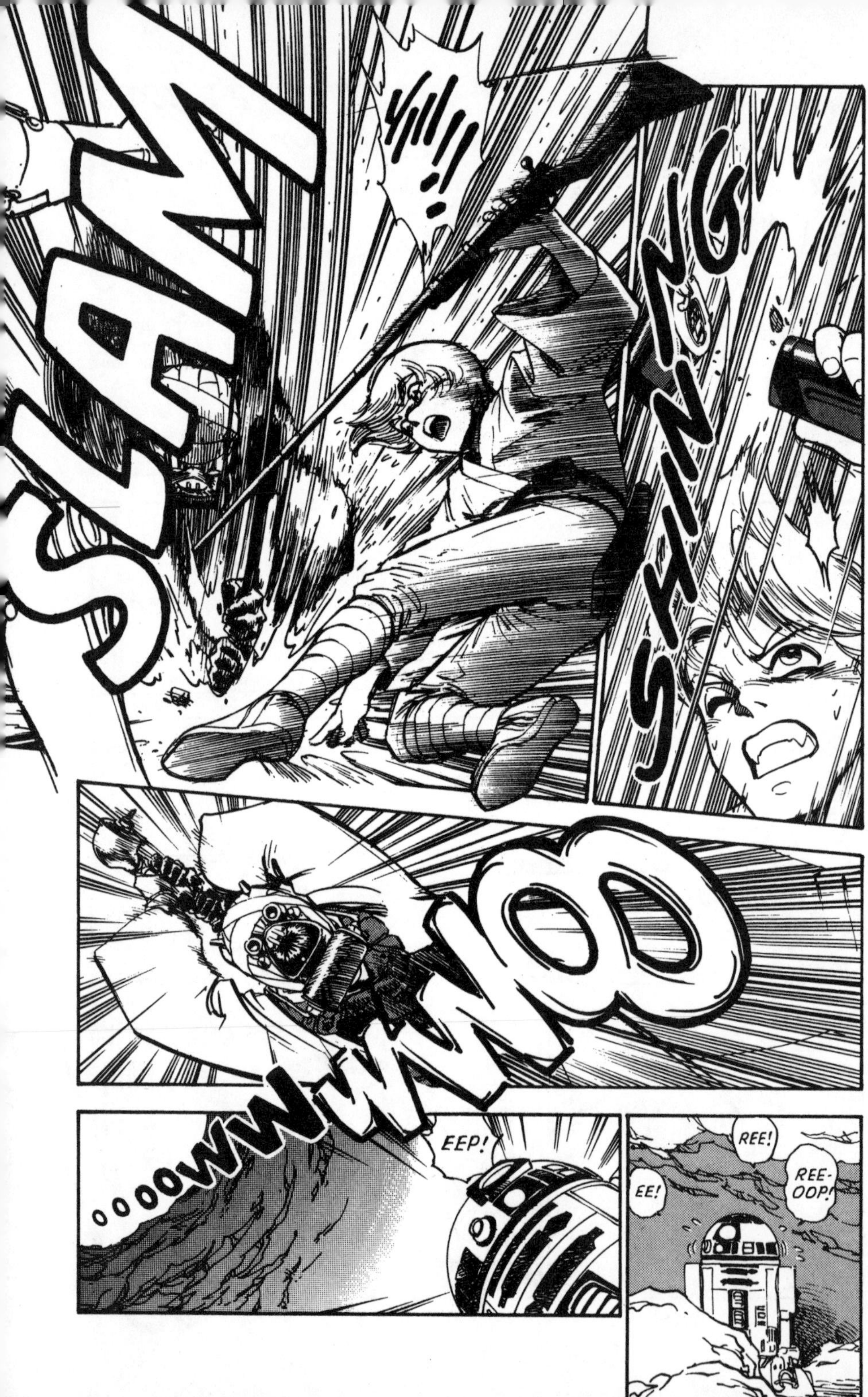
SLAM
SHING
BWWWWoooo...
EEP!
REE!
EE!
REE-OOP!

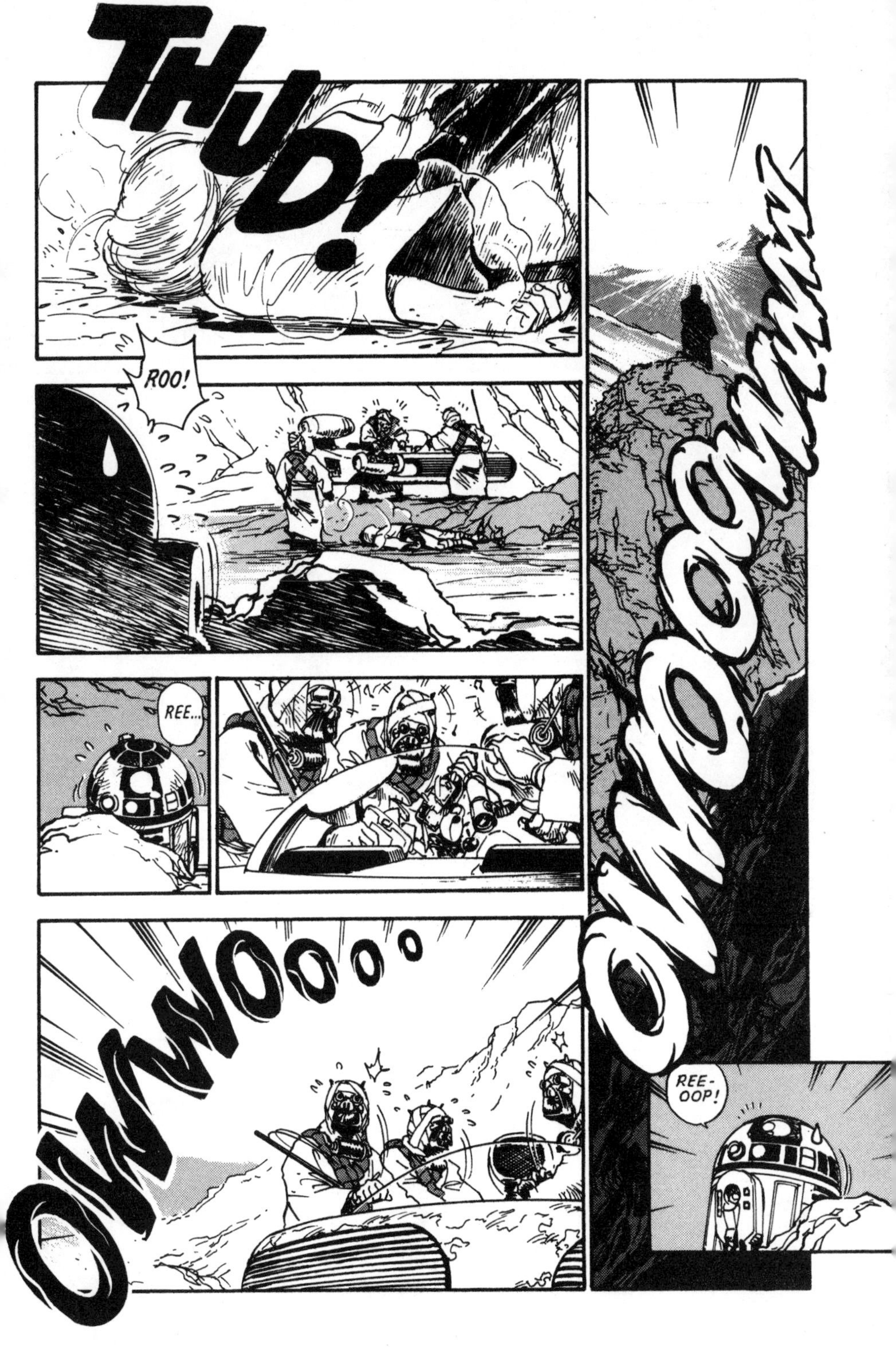
THUD!
ROO!
REE...
OWWOOooo
OWWOOOOWWWW
REE-OOP!

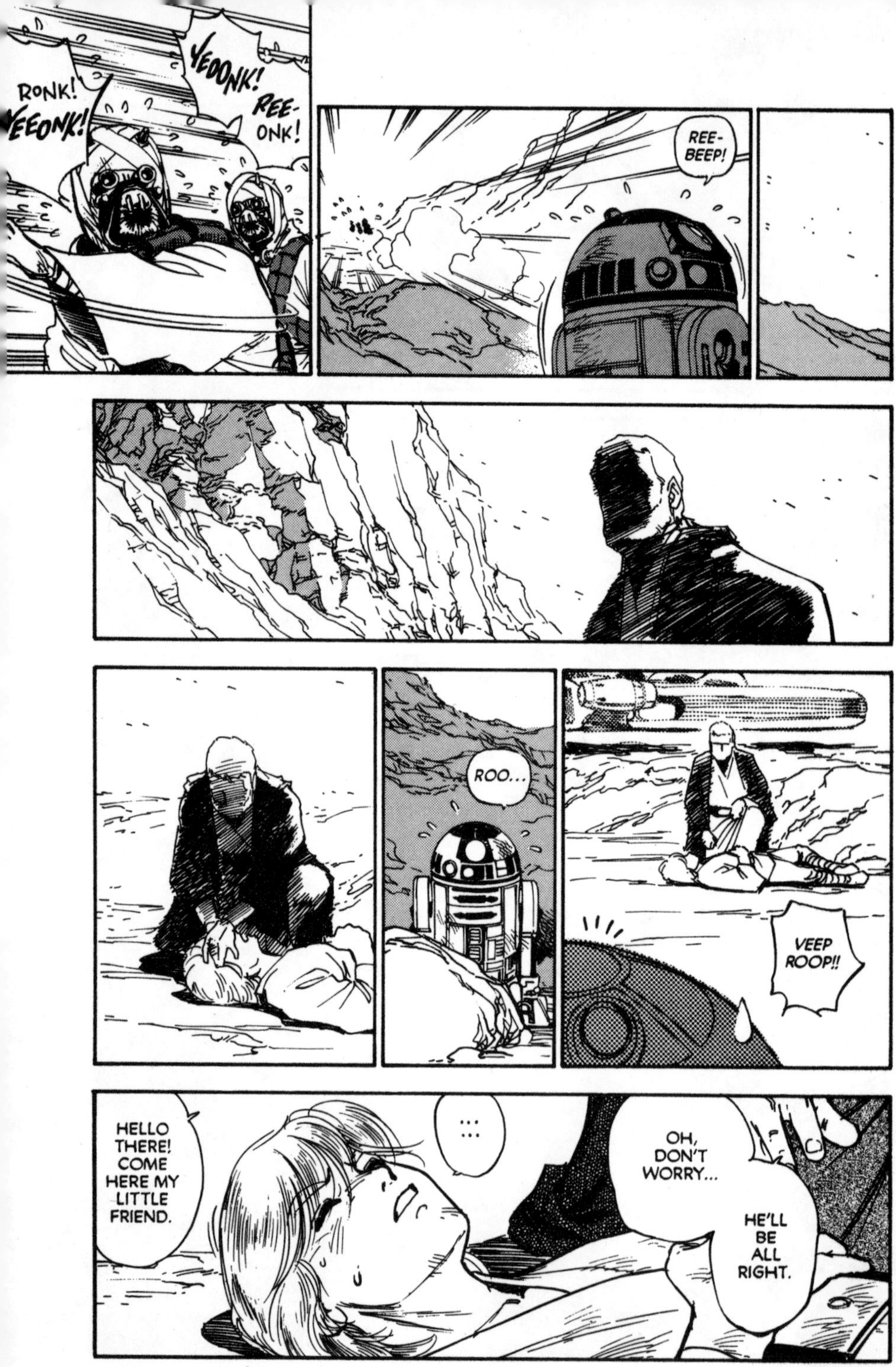

RONK!
YEEONK!
YEOONK!
REE-ONK!
REE-BEEP!
ROO...
VEEP ROOP!!
HELLO THERE! COME HERE MY LITTLE FRIEND.
...
OH, DON'T WORRY...
HE'LL BE ALL RIGHT.

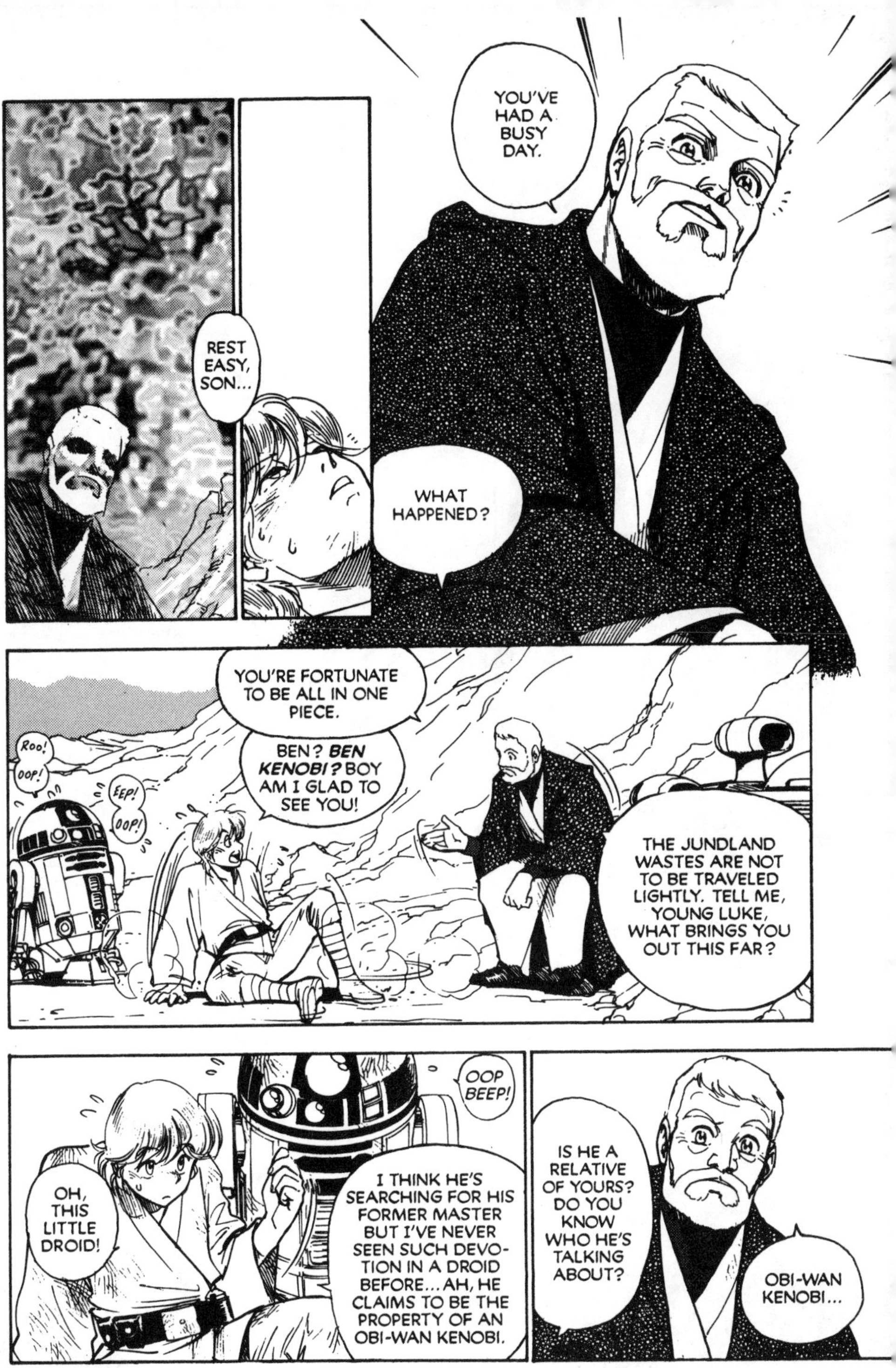
REST EASY, SON...
YOU'VE HAD A BUSY DAY.
WHAT HAPPENED?
YOU'RE FORTUNATE TO BE ALL IN ONE PIECE.
ROO! OOP!
EEP! OOP!
BEN? BEN KENOBI? BOY AM I GLAD TO SEE YOU!
THE JUNDLAND WASTES ARE NOT TO BE TRAVELED LIGHTLY. TELL ME, YOUNG LUKE, WHAT BRINGS YOU OUT THIS FAR?
OOP BEEP!
OH, THIS LITTLE DROID!
I THINK HE'S SEARCHING FOR HIS FORMER MASTER BUT I'VE NEVER SEEN SUCH DEVOTION IN A DROID BEFORE... AH, HE CLAIMS TO BE THE PROPERTY OF AN OBI-WAN KENOBI.
IS HE A RELATIVE OF YOURS? DO YOU KNOW WHO HE'S TALKING ABOUT?
OBI-WAN KENOBI...

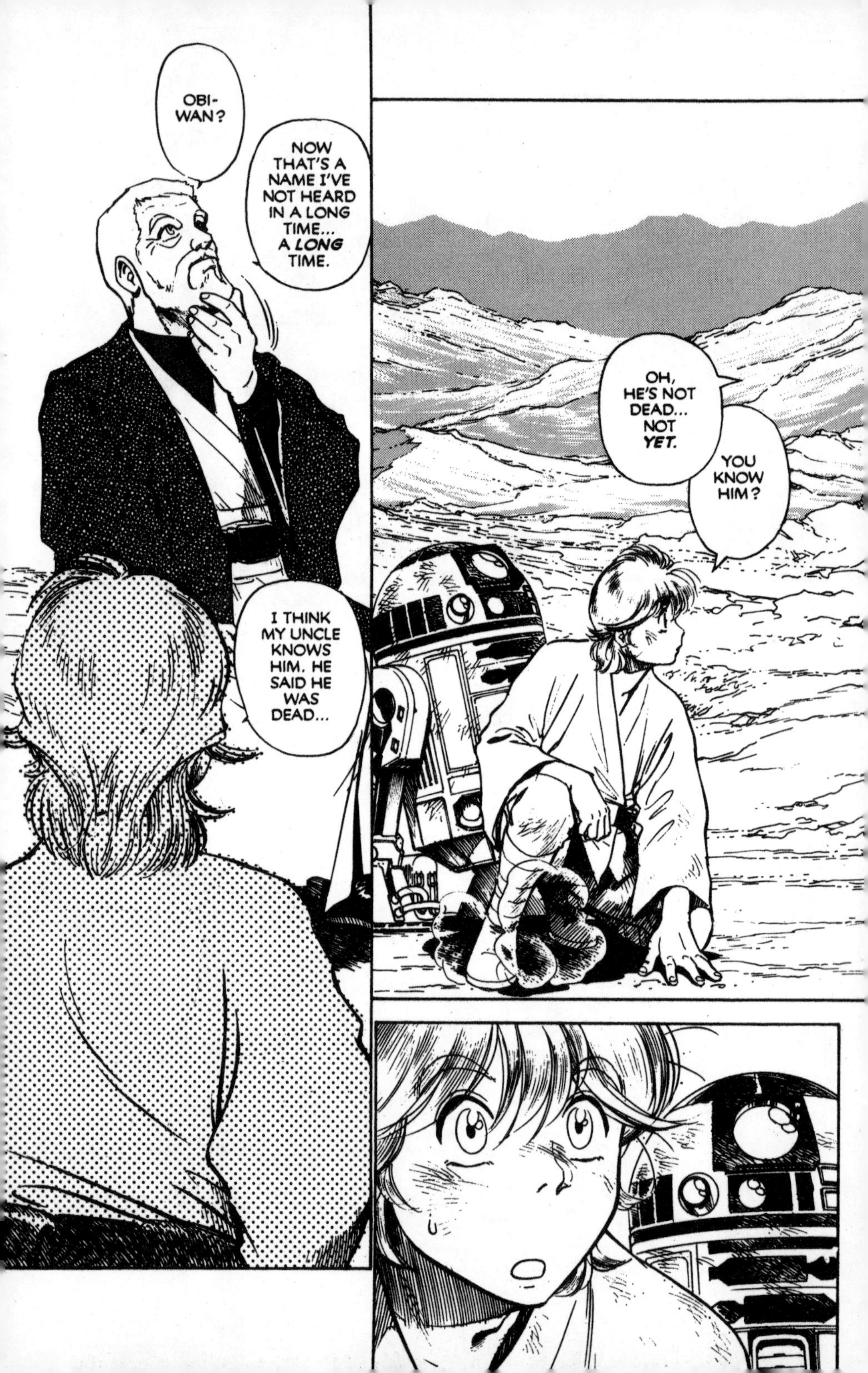
OBI-WAN?
NOW THAT'S A NAME I'VE NOT HEARD IN A LONG TIME... A *LONG* TIME.
I THINK MY UNCLE KNOWS HIM. HE SAID HE WAS DEAD...
OH, HE'S NOT DEAD... NOT *YET.*
YOU KNOW HIM?

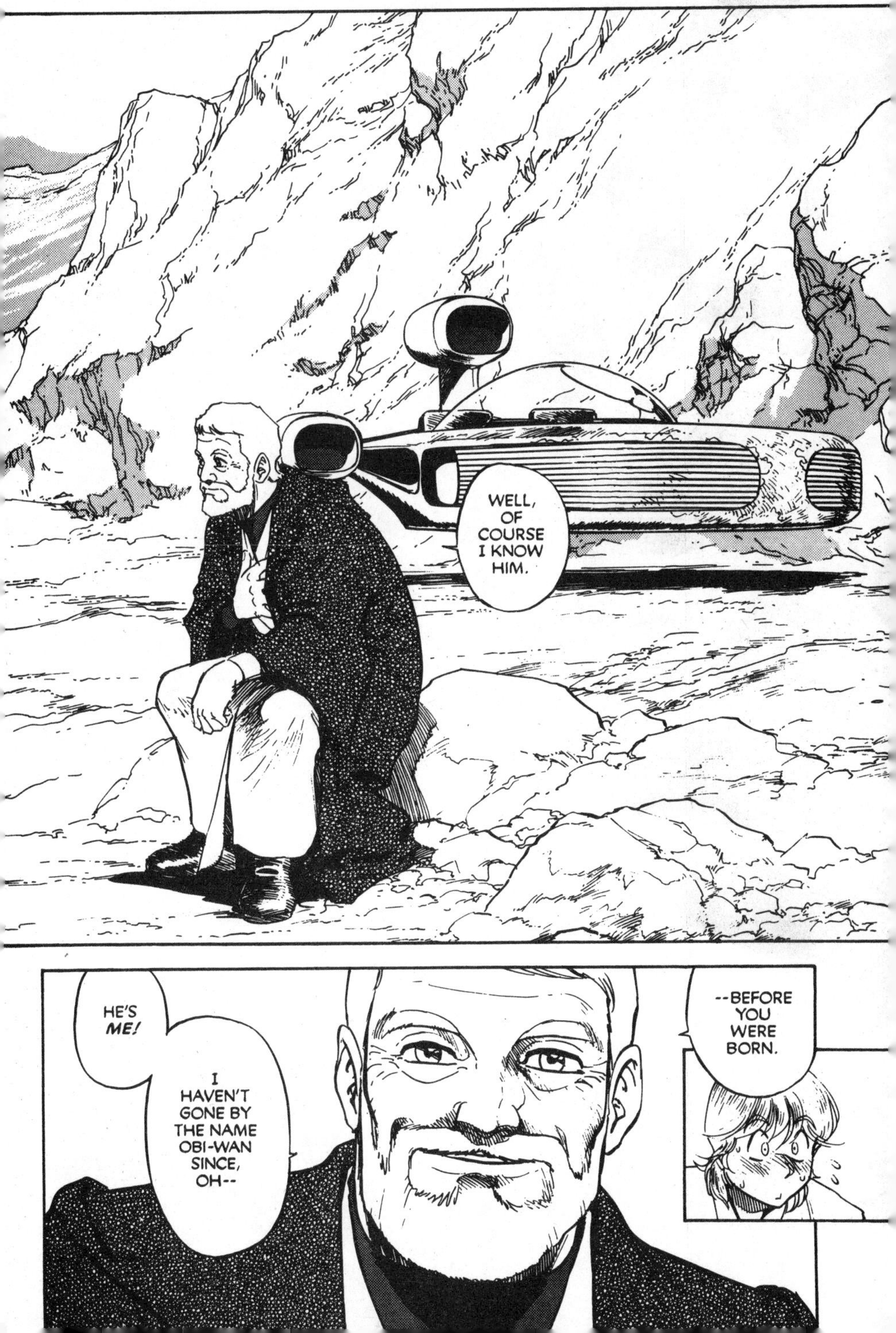
WELL, OF COURSE I KNOW HIM.
HE'S *ME!*
I HAVEN'T GONE BY THE NAME OBI-WAN SINCE, OH--
--BEFORE YOU WERE BORN.

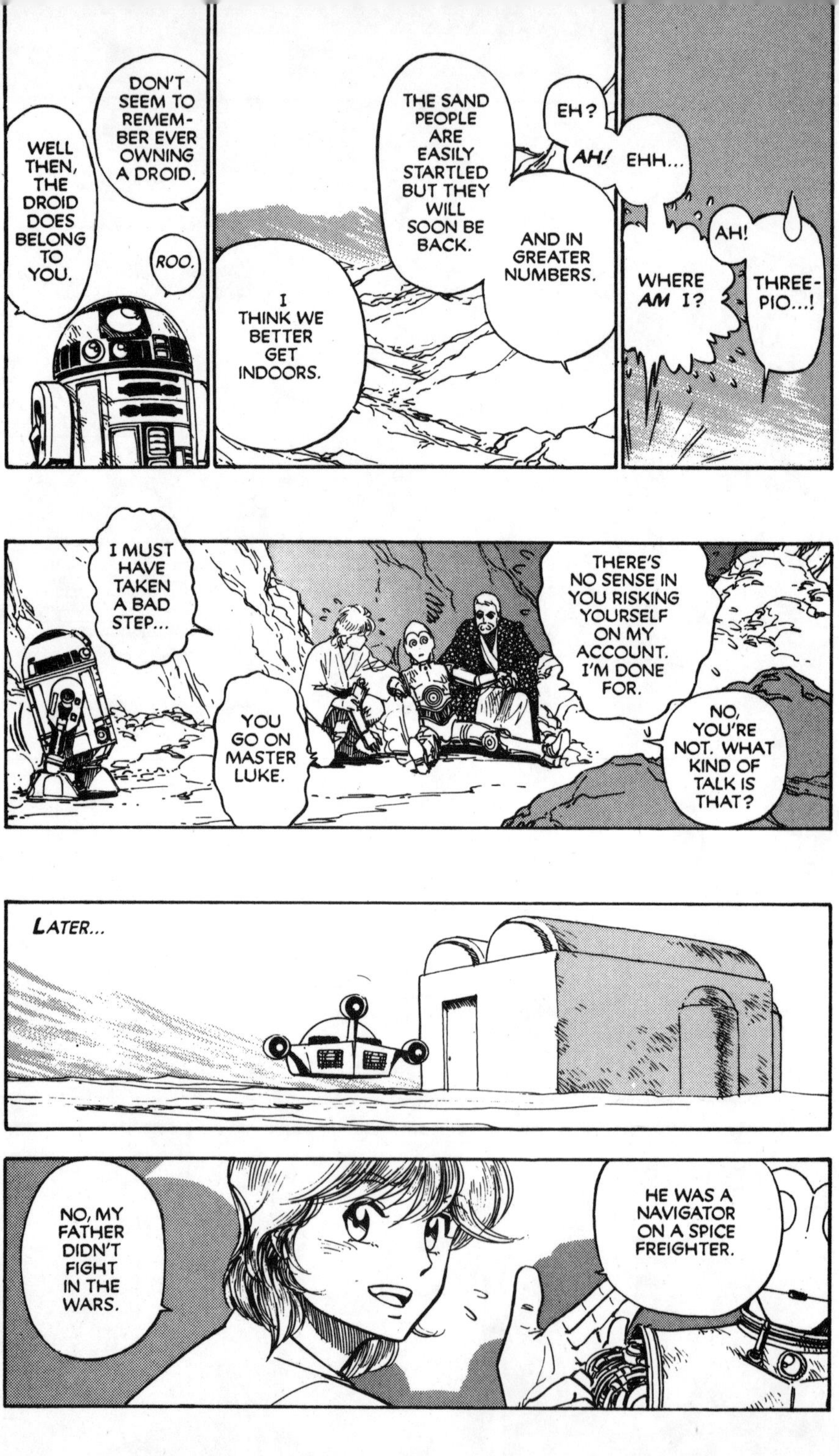
WELL THEN, THE DROID DOES BELONG TO YOU.
DON'T SEEM TO REMEMBER EVER OWNING A DROID.
ROO.
I THINK WE BETTER GET INDOORS.
THE SAND PEOPLE ARE EASILY STARTLED BUT THEY WILL SOON BE BACK.
AND IN GREATER NUMBERS.
EH?
AH!
EHH...
THREE-PIO...!
AH!
WHERE AM I?
I MUST HAVE TAKEN A BAD STEP...
YOU GO ON MASTER LUKE.
THERE'S NO SENSE IN YOU RISKING YOURSELF ON MY ACCOUNT. I'M DONE FOR.
NO, YOU'RE NOT. WHAT KIND OF TALK IS THAT?
LATER...
NO, MY FATHER DIDN'T FIGHT IN THE WARS.
HE WAS A NAVIGATOR ON A SPICE FREIGHTER.

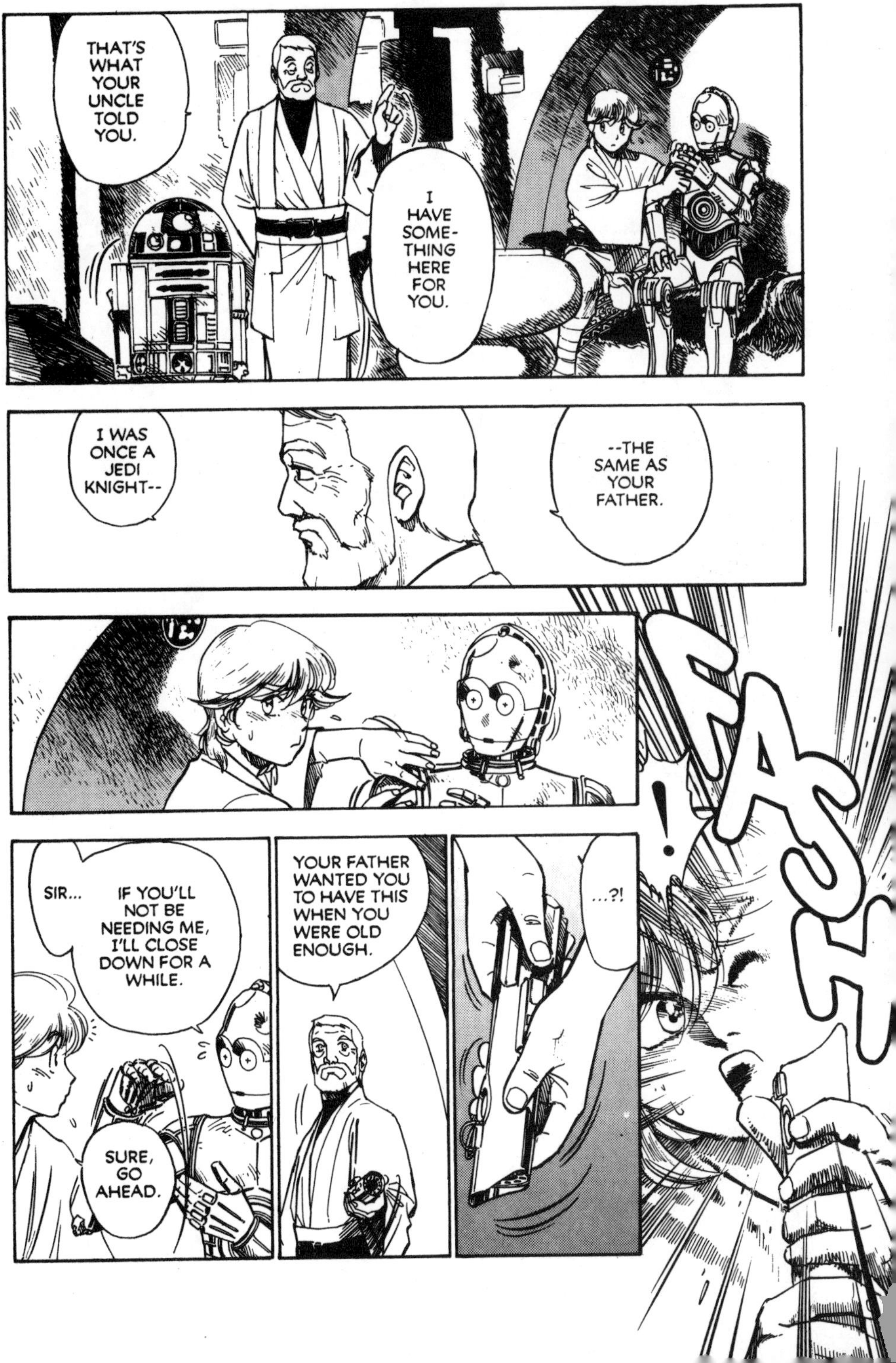
THAT'S WHAT YOUR UNCLE TOLD YOU.
I HAVE SOMETHING HERE FOR YOU.
I WAS ONCE A JEDI KNIGHT--
--THE SAME AS YOUR FATHER.
SIR...
IF YOU'LL NOT BE NEEDING ME, I'LL CLOSE DOWN FOR A WHILE.
SURE, GO AHEAD.
YOUR FATHER WANTED YOU TO HAVE THIS WHEN YOU WERE OLD ENOUGH.
...?!
!

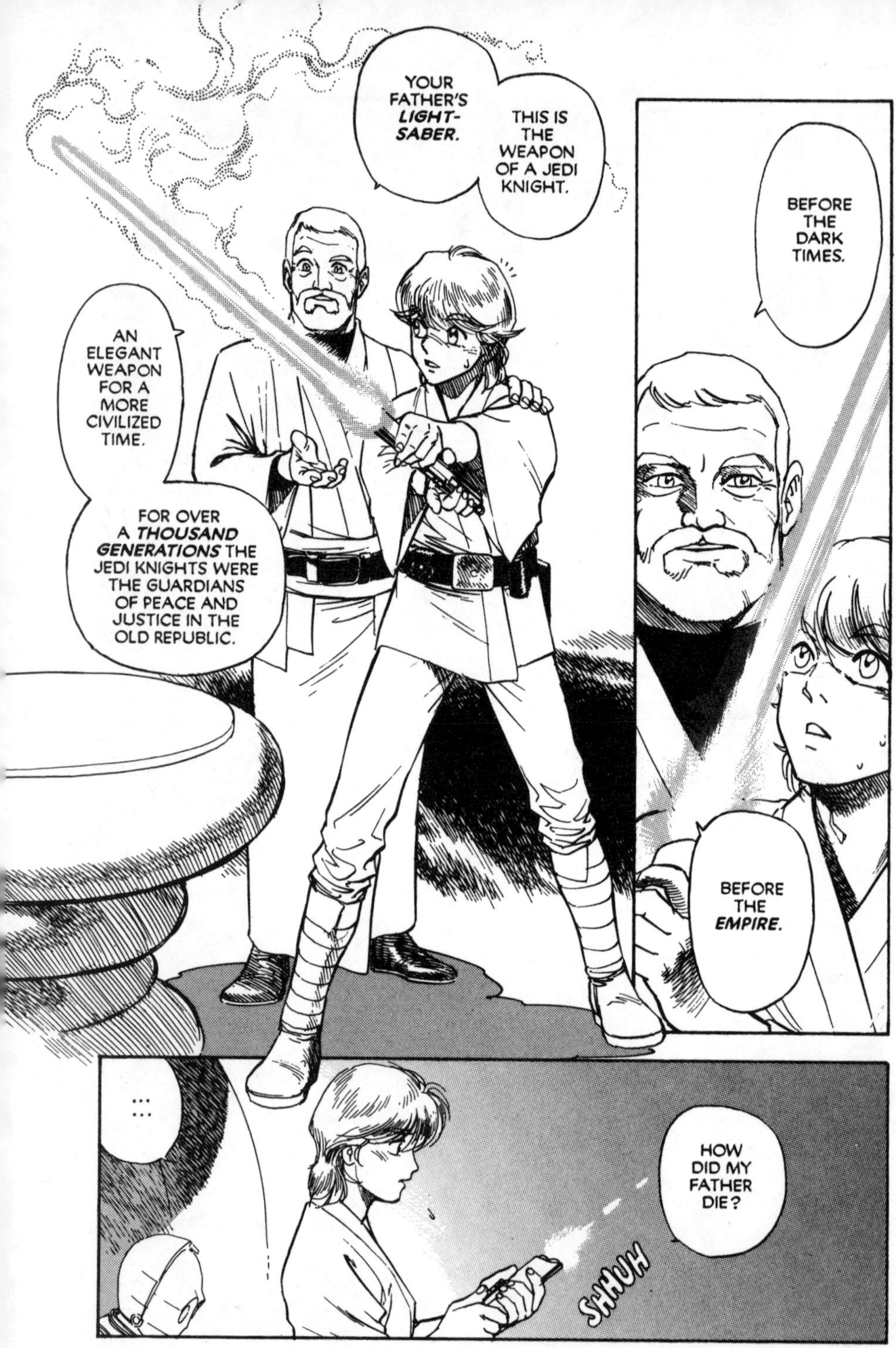
YOUR FATHER'S *LIGHT-SABER.*
THIS IS THE WEAPON OF A JEDI KNIGHT.
AN ELEGANT WEAPON FOR A MORE CIVILIZED TIME.
FOR OVER A ***THOUSAND GENERATIONS*** THE JEDI KNIGHTS WERE THE GUARDIANS OF PEACE AND JUSTICE IN THE OLD REPUBLIC.
BEFORE THE DARK TIMES.
BEFORE THE ***EMPIRE.***
... ...
HOW DID MY FATHER DIE?
SHHUH

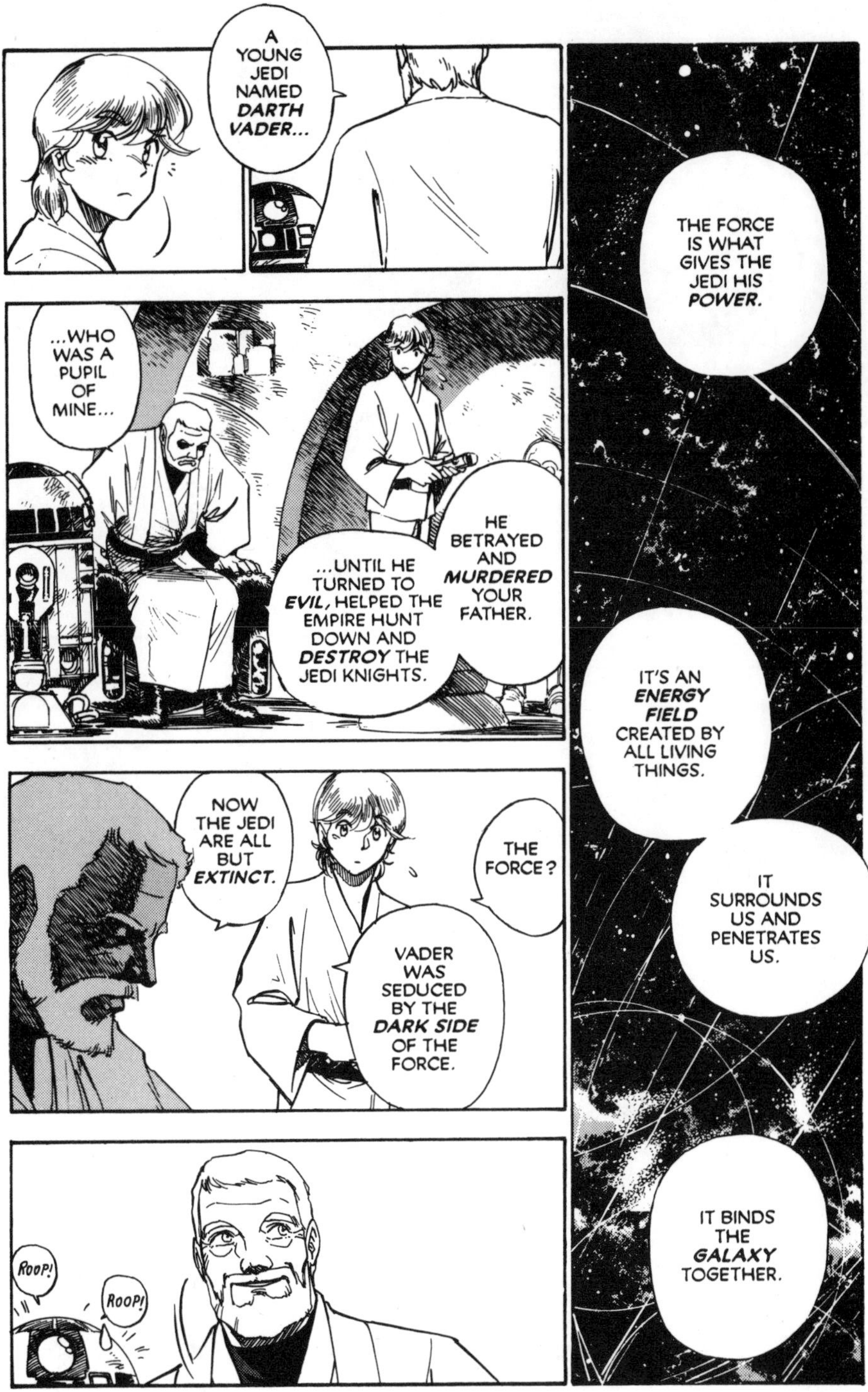
A YOUNG JEDI NAMED DARTH VADER...
...WHO WAS A PUPIL OF MINE...
...UNTIL HE TURNED TO EVIL, HELPED THE EMPIRE HUNT DOWN AND DESTROY THE JEDI KNIGHTS.
HE BETRAYED AND MURDERED YOUR FATHER.
NOW THE JEDI ARE ALL BUT EXTINCT.
THE FORCE?
VADER WAS SEDUCED BY THE DARK SIDE OF THE FORCE.
ROOP!
ROOP!
THE FORCE IS WHAT GIVES THE JEDI HIS POWER.
IT'S AN ENERGY FIELD CREATED BY ALL LIVING THINGS.
IT SURROUNDS US AND PENETRATES US.
IT BINDS THE GALAXY TOGETHER.

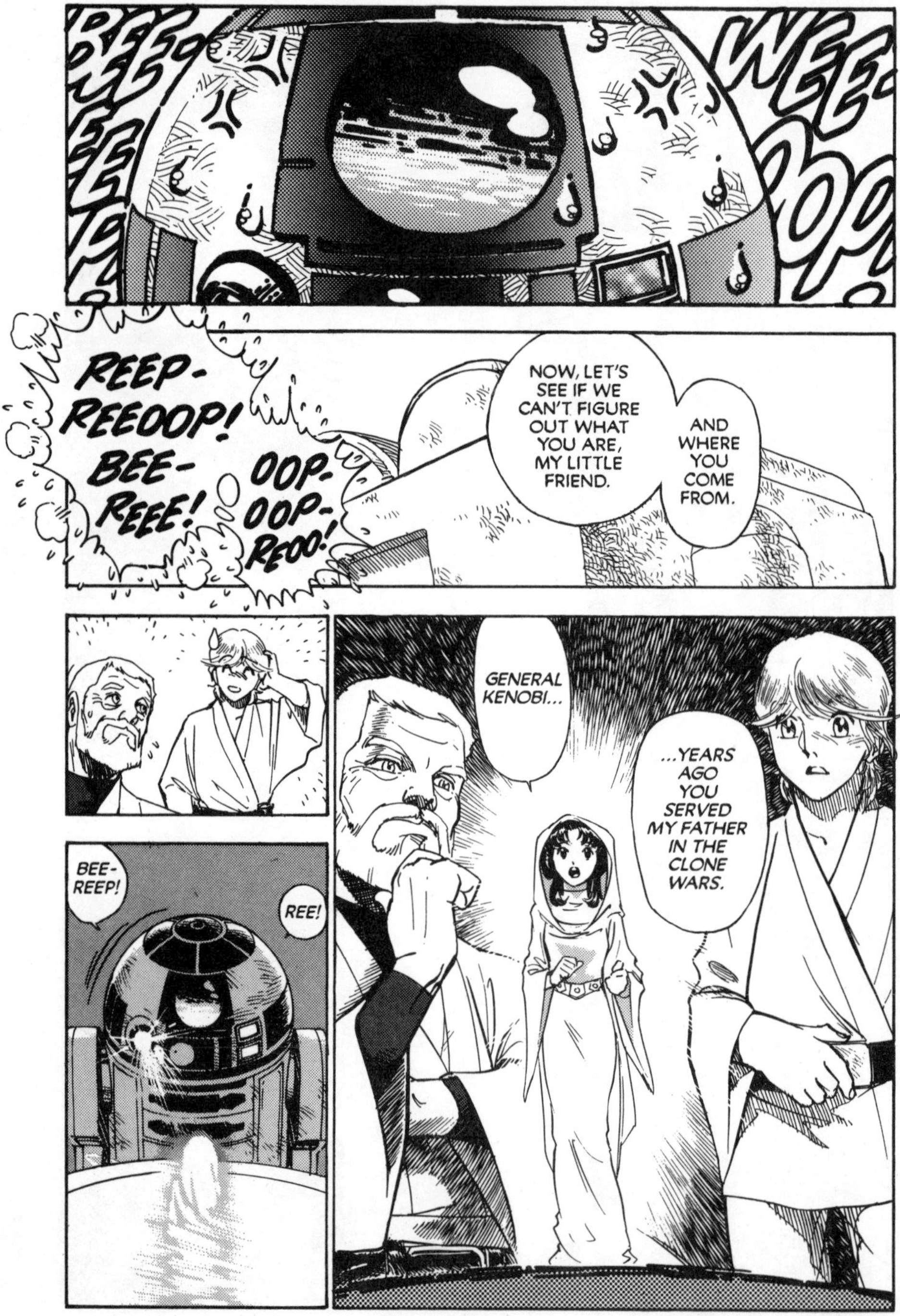
REEP-REEOOP!
BEE-REEE!
OOP-OOP-REOO!
NOW, LET'S SEE IF WE CAN'T FIGURE OUT WHAT YOU ARE, MY LITTLE FRIEND.
AND WHERE YOU COME FROM.
BEE-REEP!
REE!
GENERAL KENOBI...
...YEARS AGO YOU SERVED MY FATHER IN THE CLONE WARS.

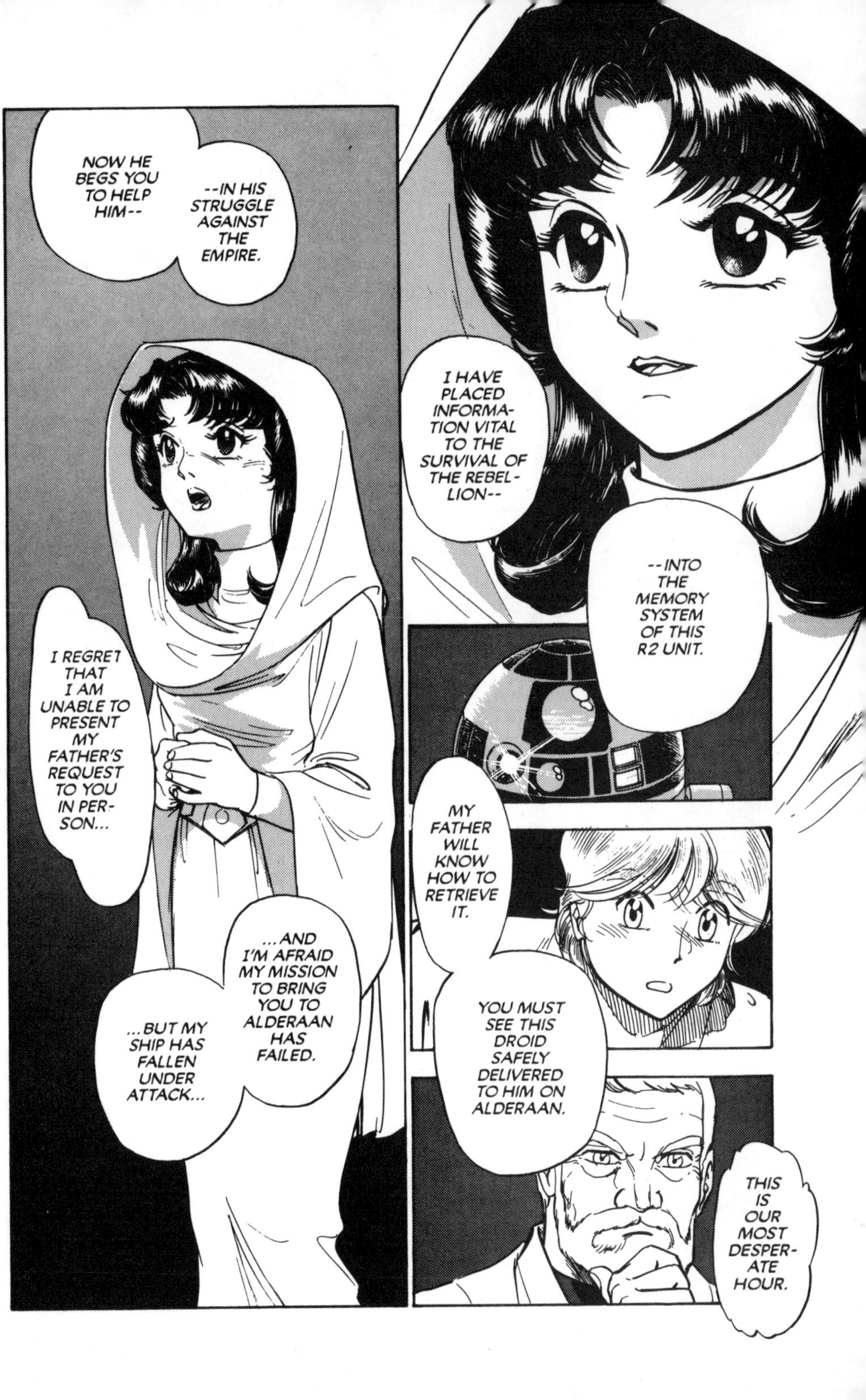
NOW HE BEGS YOU TO HELP HIM--
--IN HIS STRUGGLE AGAINST THE EMPIRE.
I REGRET THAT I AM UNABLE TO PRESENT MY FATHER'S REQUEST TO YOU IN PER-SON...
...BUT MY SHIP HAS FALLEN UNDER ATTACK...
...AND I'M AFRAID MY MISSION TO BRING YOU TO ALDERAAN HAS FAILED.
I HAVE PLACED INFORMA-TION VITAL TO THE SURVIVAL OF THE REBEL-LION--
--INTO THE MEMORY SYSTEM OF THIS R2 UNIT.
MY FATHER WILL KNOW HOW TO RETRIEVE IT.
YOU MUST SEE THIS DROID SAFELY DELIVERED TO HIM ON ALDERAAN.
THIS IS OUR MOST DESPERATE HOUR.

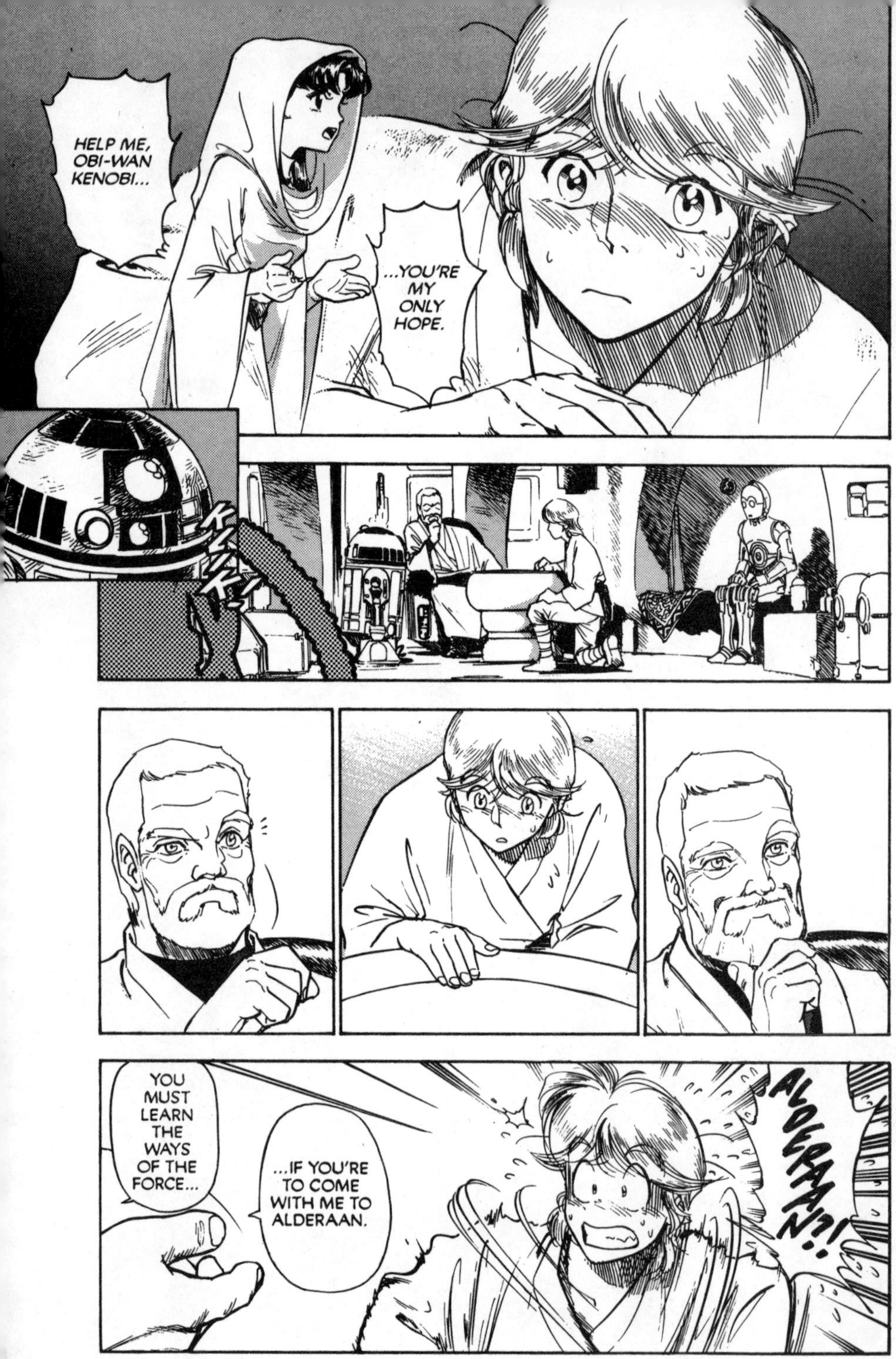
HELP ME, OBI-WAN KENOBI...
...YOU'RE MY ONLY HOPE.
KLIK!
YOU MUST LEARN THE WAYS OF THE FORCE...
...IF YOU'RE TO COME WITH ME TO ALDERAAN.
ALDERAAN?!

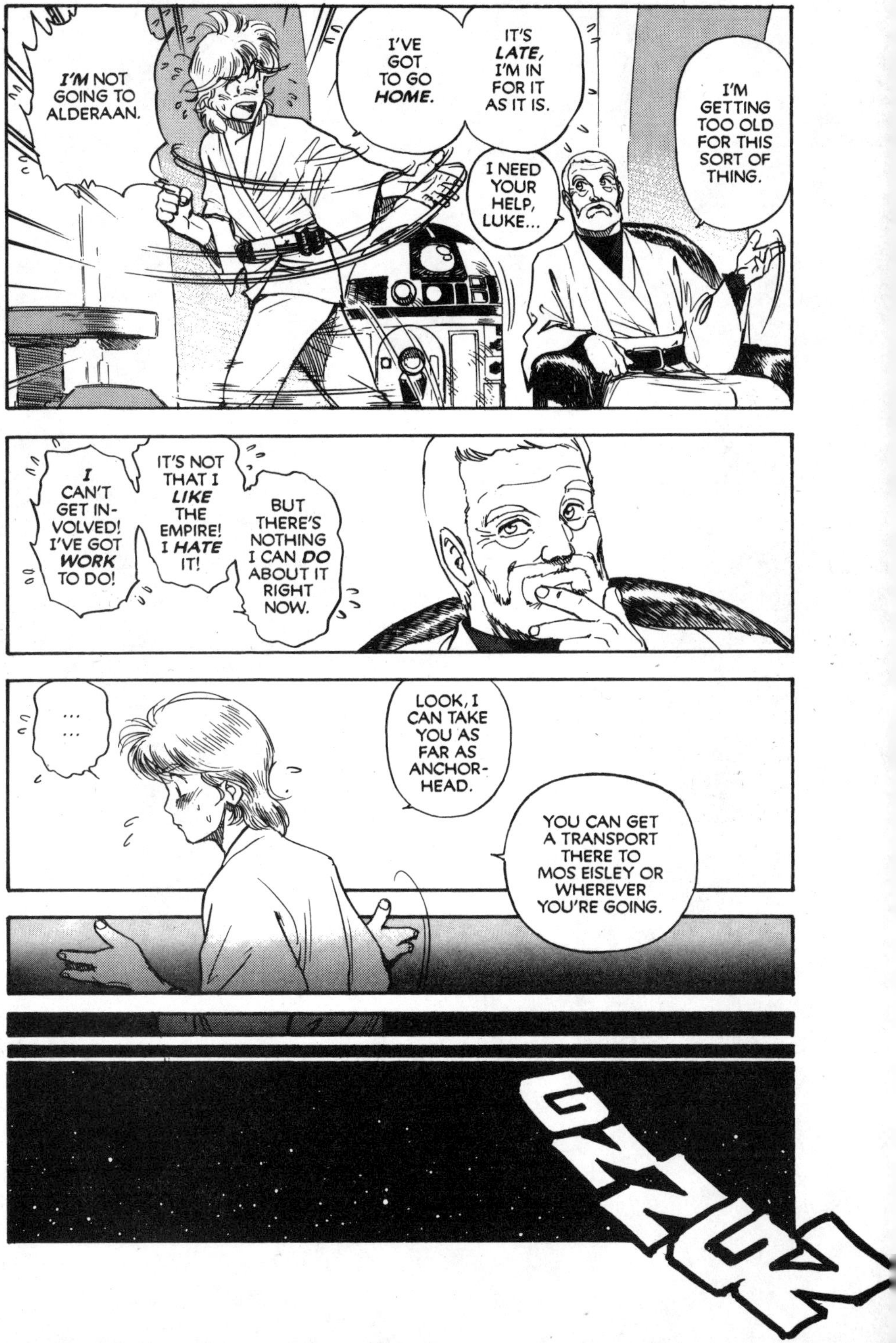
I'M NOT GOING TO ALDERAAN.
I'VE GOT TO GO HOME.
IT'S LATE, I'M IN FOR IT AS IT IS.
I NEED YOUR HELP, LUKE...
I'M GETTING TOO OLD FOR THIS SORT OF THING.
I CAN'T GET IN-VOLVED! I'VE GOT WORK TO DO!
IT'S NOT THAT I LIKE THE EMPIRE! I HATE IT!
BUT THERE'S NOTHING I CAN DO ABOUT IT RIGHT NOW.
... ...
LOOK, I CAN TAKE YOU AS FAR AS ANCHOR-HEAD.
YOU CAN GET A TRANSPORT THERE TO MOS EISLEY OR WHEREVER YOU'RE GOING.

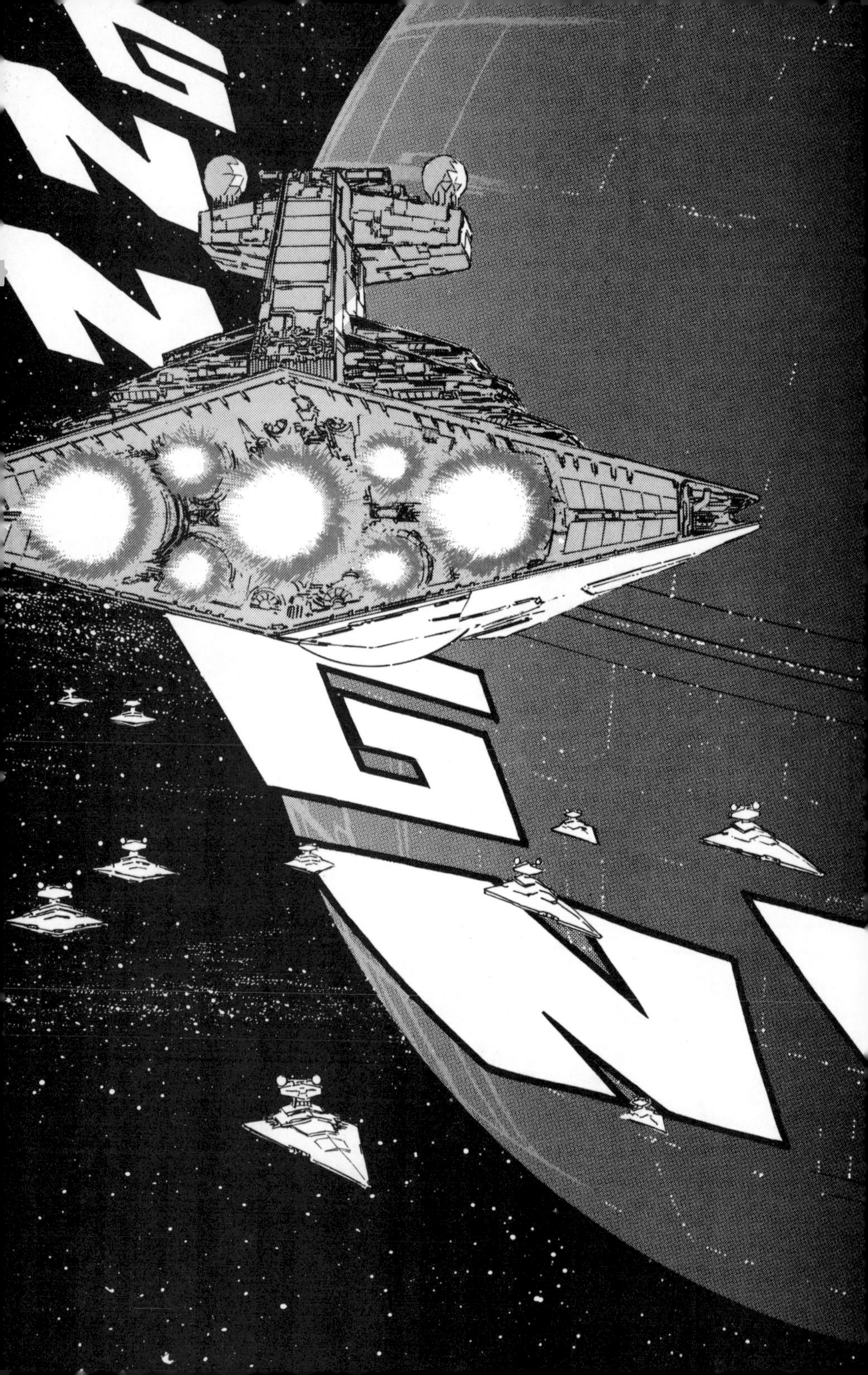

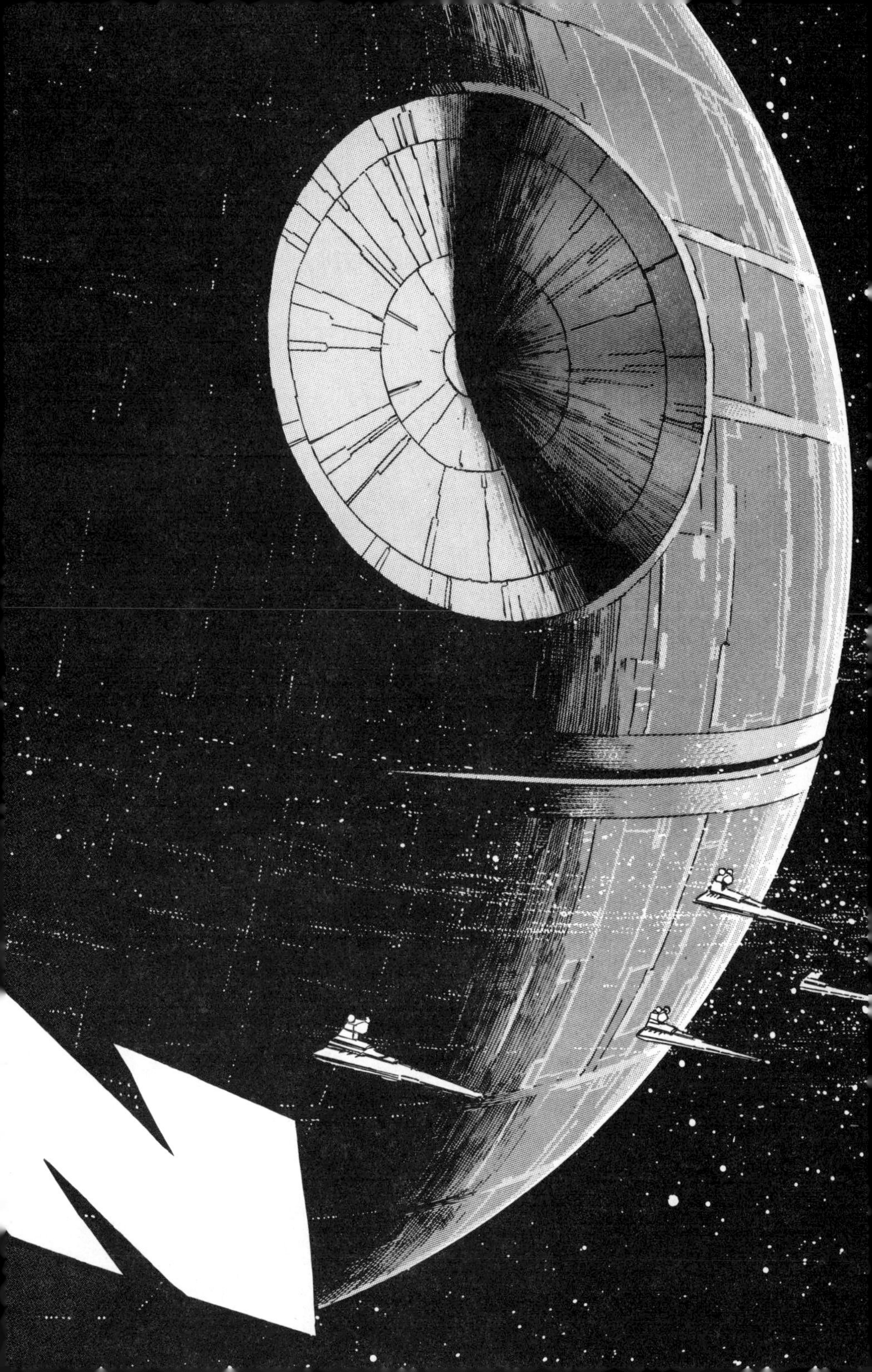

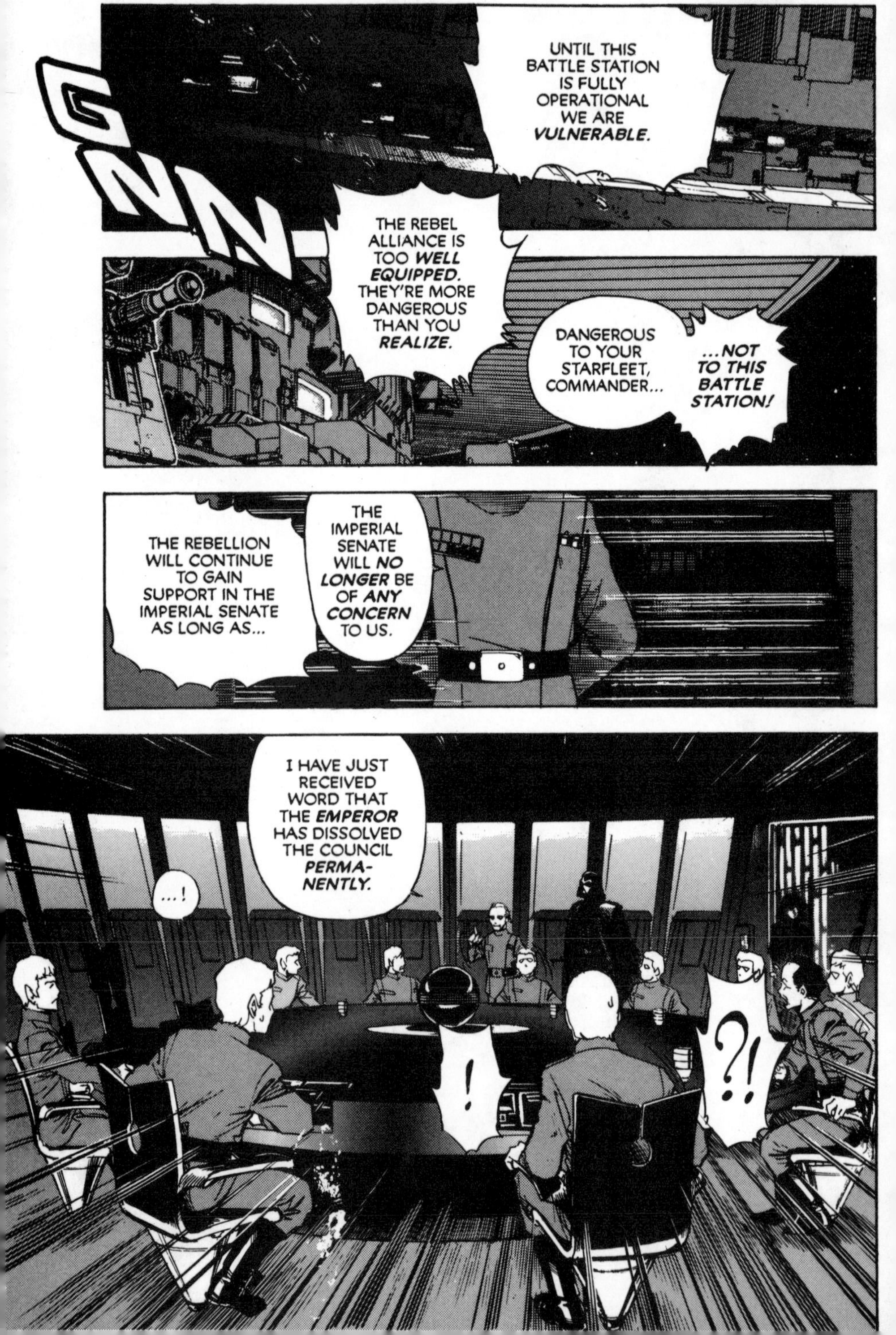
GNN
UNTIL THIS BATTLE STATION IS FULLY OPERATIONAL WE ARE *VULNERABLE.*
THE REBEL ALLIANCE IS TOO *WELL EQUIPPED.* THEY'RE MORE DANGEROUS THAN YOU *REALIZE.*
DANGEROUS TO YOUR STARFLEET, COMMANDER...
...NOT TO THIS BATTLE STATION!
THE REBELLION WILL CONTINUE TO GAIN SUPPORT IN THE IMPERIAL SENATE AS LONG AS...
THE IMPERIAL SENATE WILL *NO LONGER* BE OF *ANY CONCERN* TO US.
I HAVE JUST RECEIVED WORD THAT THE *EMPEROR* HAS DISSOLVED THE COUNCIL *PERMA-NENTLY.*
...!
!
?!

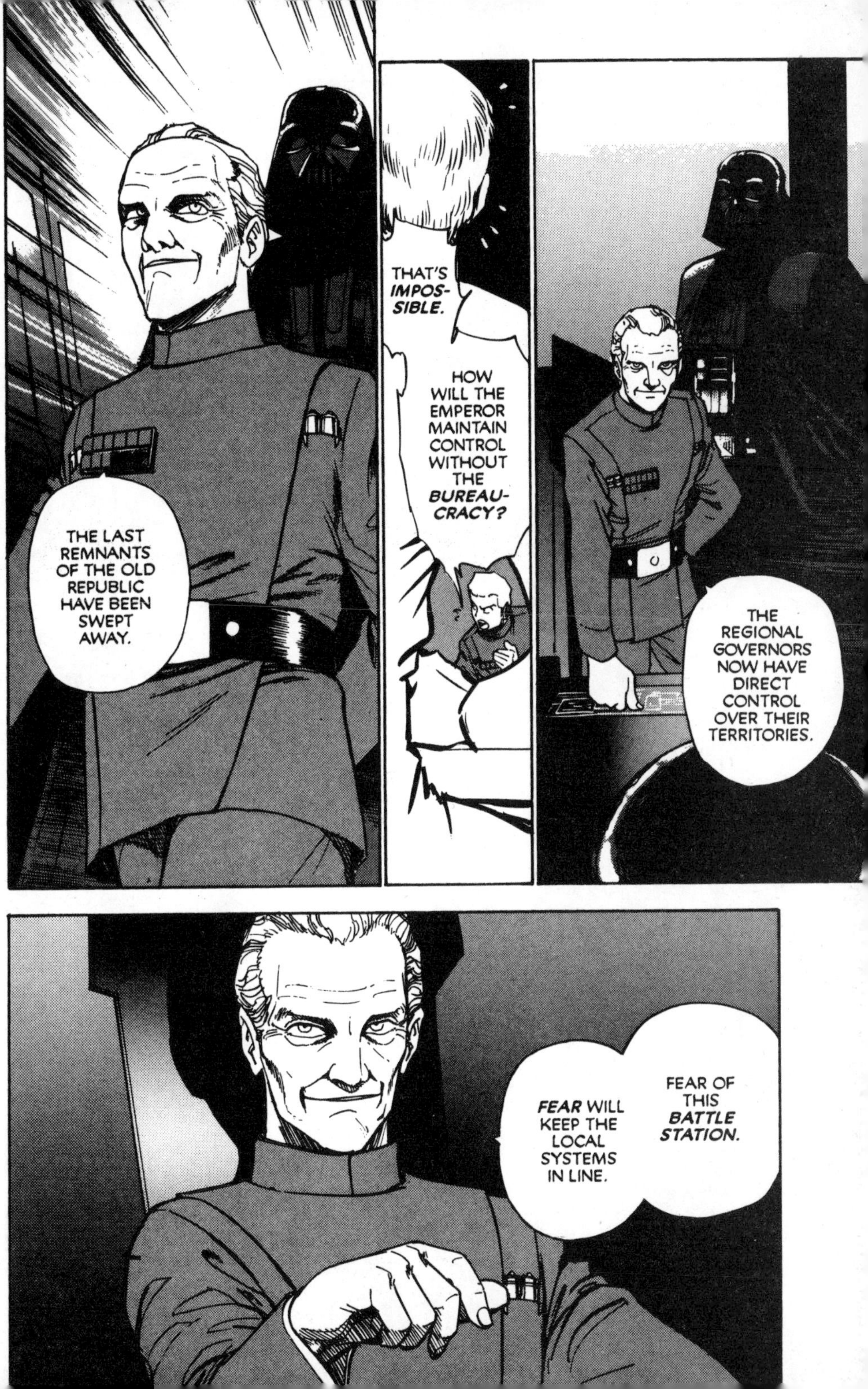
THE LAST REMNANTS OF THE OLD REPUBLIC HAVE BEEN SWEPT AWAY.
THAT'S *IMPOSSIBLE.*
HOW WILL THE EMPEROR MAINTAIN CONTROL WITHOUT THE *BUREAUCRACY?*
THE REGIONAL GOVERNORS NOW HAVE DIRECT CONTROL OVER THEIR TERRITORIES.
FEAR WILL KEEP THE LOCAL SYSTEMS IN LINE.
FEAR OF THIS *BATTLE STATION.*

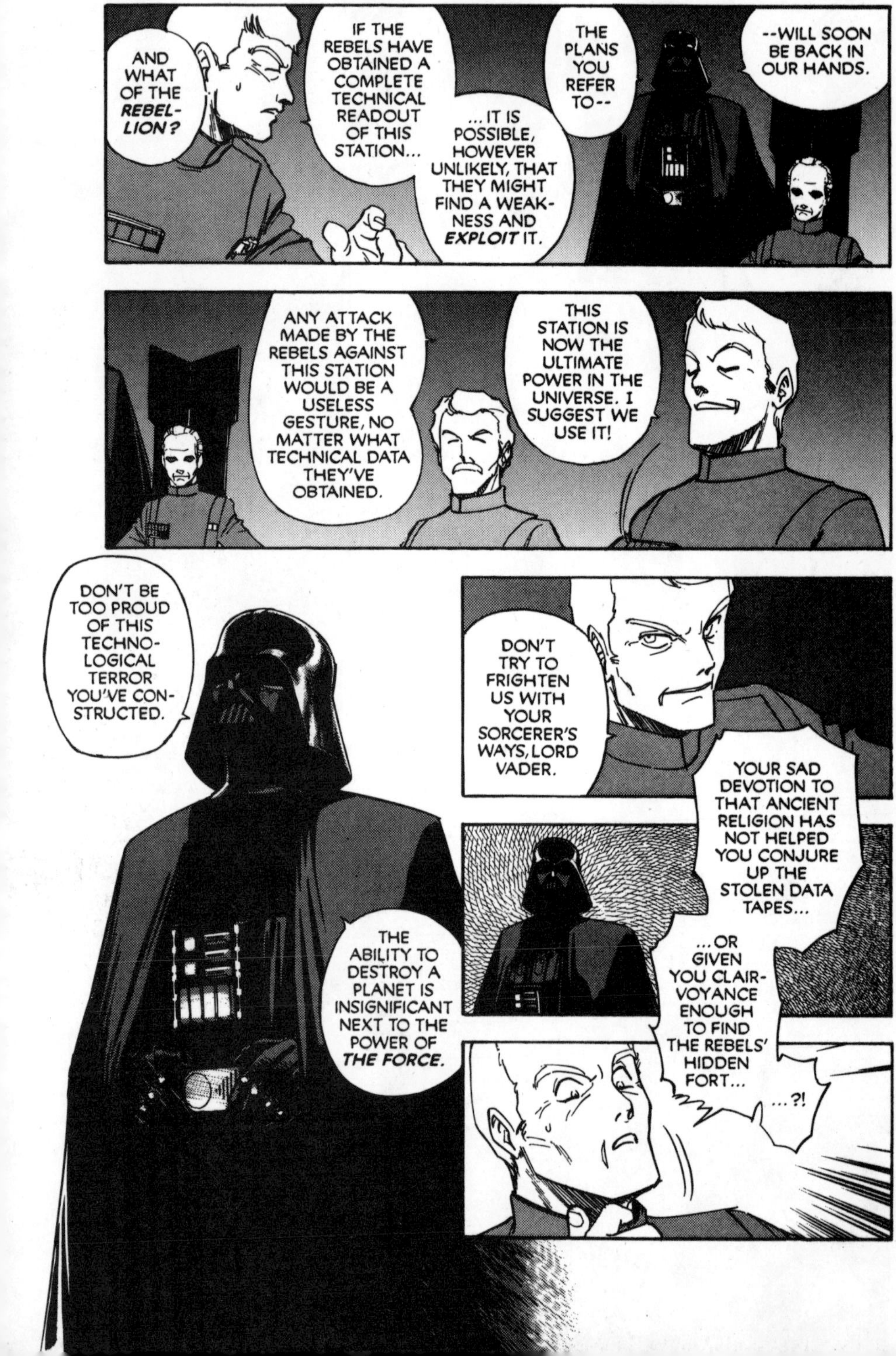
AND WHAT OF THE *REBELLION?*
IF THE REBELS HAVE OBTAINED A COMPLETE TECHNICAL READOUT OF THIS STATION...
...IT IS POSSIBLE, HOWEVER UNLIKELY, THAT THEY MIGHT FIND A WEAKNESS AND *EXPLOIT* IT.
THE PLANS YOU REFER TO--
--WILL SOON BE BACK IN OUR HANDS.
ANY ATTACK MADE BY THE REBELS AGAINST THIS STATION WOULD BE A USELESS GESTURE, NO MATTER WHAT TECHNICAL DATA THEY'VE OBTAINED.
THIS STATION IS NOW THE ULTIMATE POWER IN THE UNIVERSE. I SUGGEST WE USE IT!
DON'T BE TOO PROUD OF THIS TECHNOLOGICAL TERROR YOU'VE CONSTRUCTED.
THE ABILITY TO DESTROY A PLANET IS INSIGNIFICANT NEXT TO THE POWER OF *THE FORCE.*
DON'T TRY TO FRIGHTEN US WITH YOUR SORCERER'S WAYS, LORD VADER.
YOUR SAD DEVOTION TO THAT ANCIENT RELIGION HAS NOT HELPED YOU CONJURE UP THE STOLEN DATA TAPES...
...OR GIVEN YOU CLAIRVOYANCE ENOUGH TO FIND THE REBELS' HIDDEN FORT...
...?!

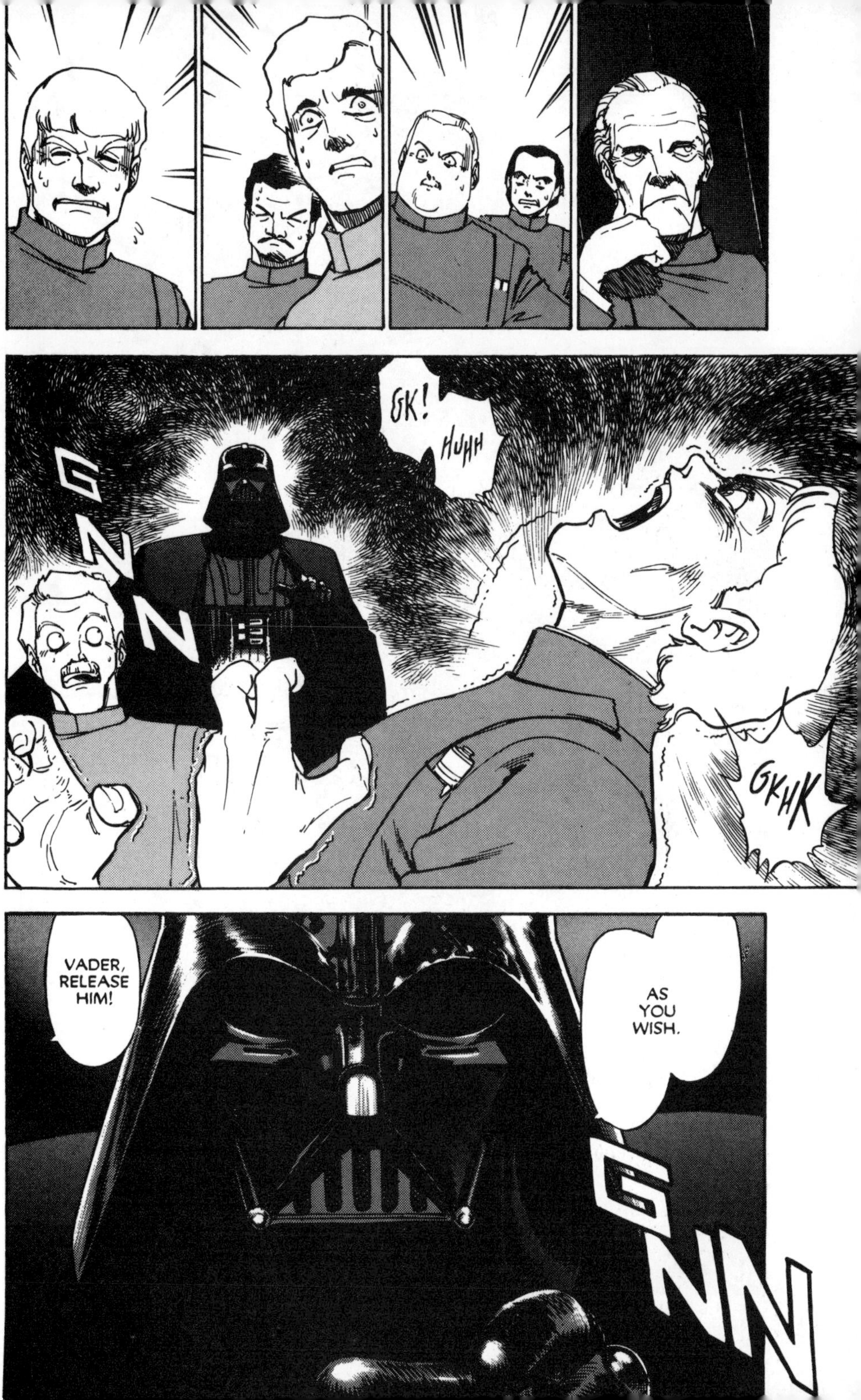
GK!
HUHH
GNN
GKHK
VADER, RELEASE HIM!
AS YOU WISH.
GNN

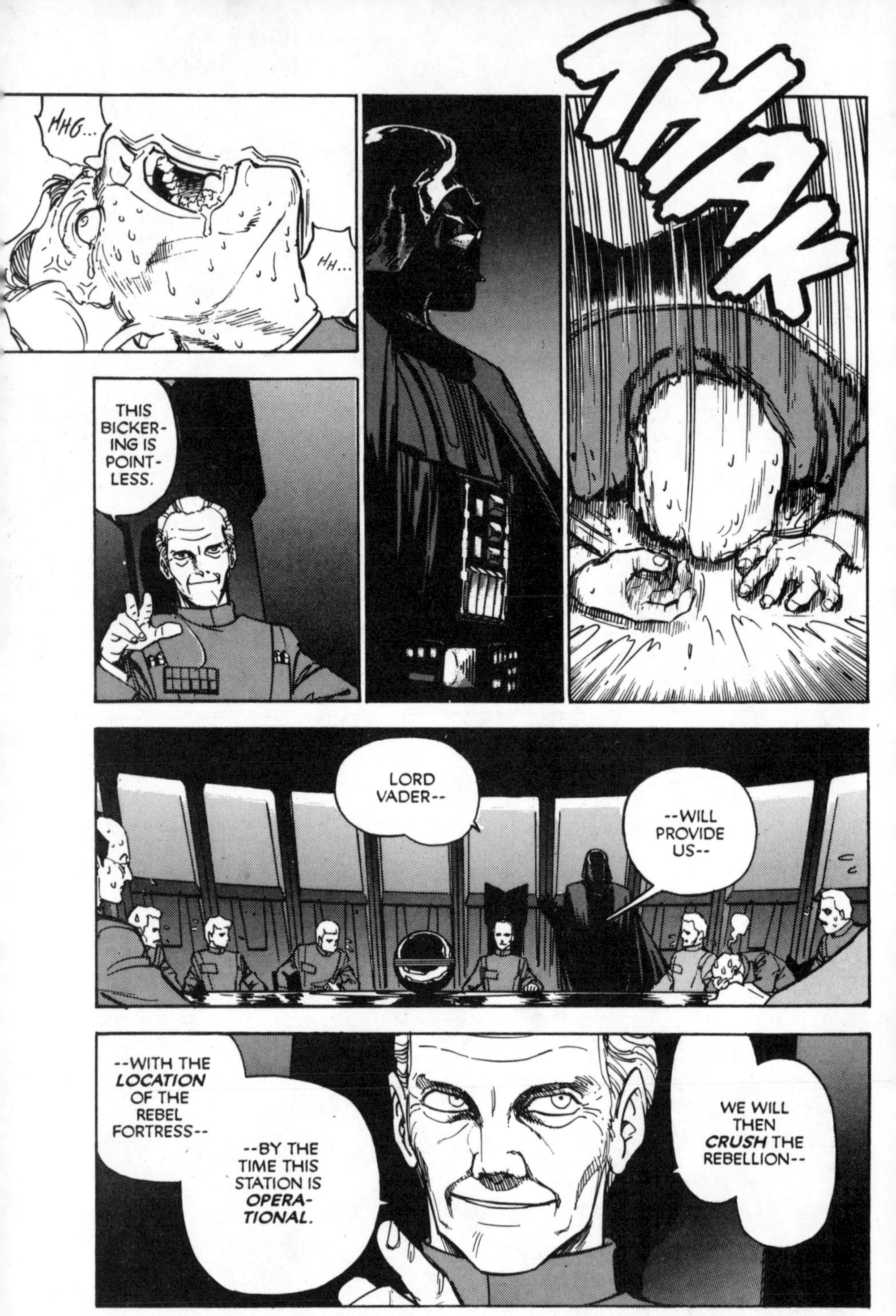

MHG...
HH...
THIS BICKERING IS POINTLESS.
THAK
LORD VADER--
--WILL PROVIDE US--
--WITH THE LOCATION OF THE REBEL FORTRESS--
--BY THE TIME THIS STATION IS OPERATIONAL.
WE WILL THEN CRUSH THE REBELLION--

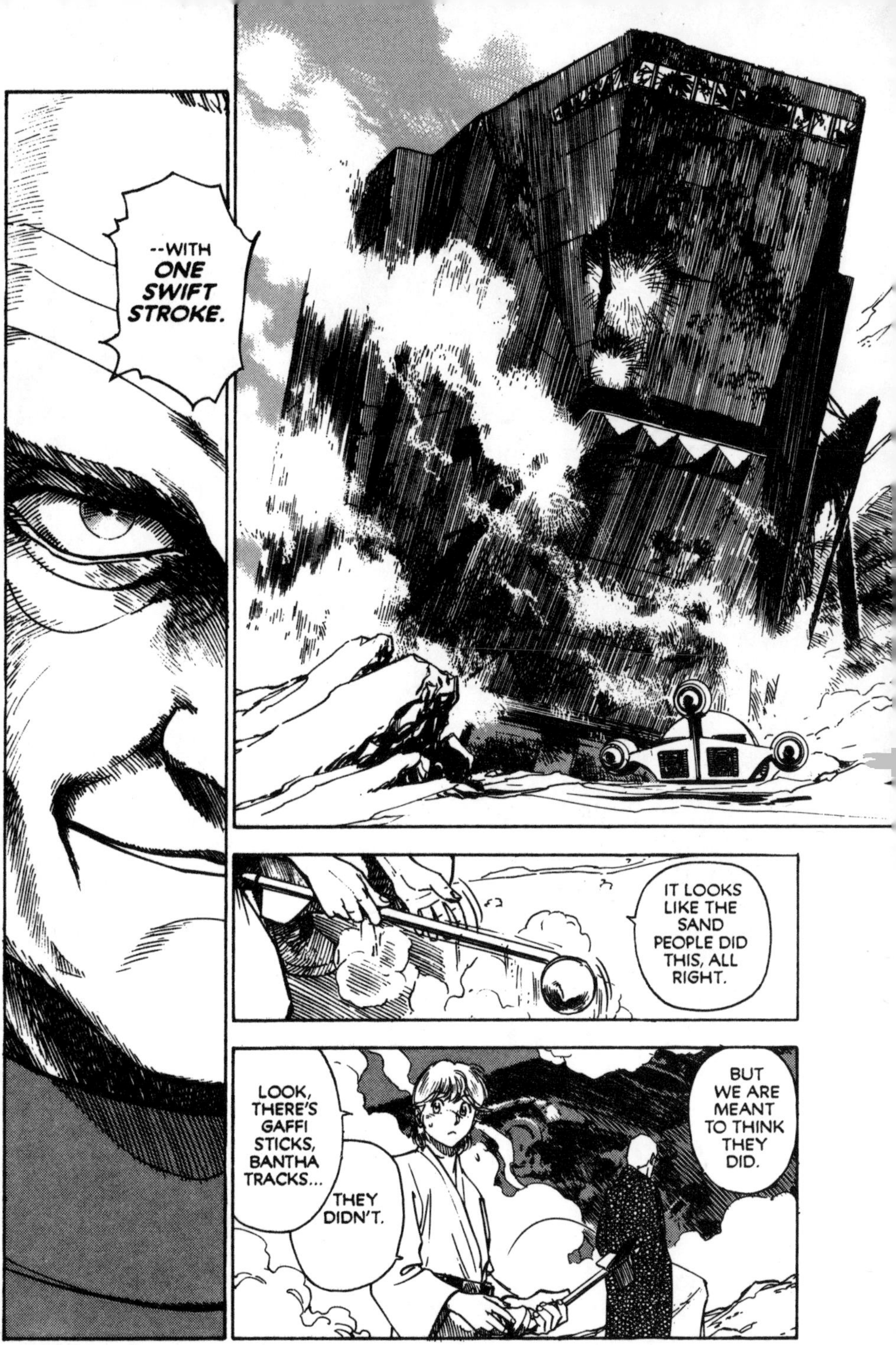
--WITH ONE SWIFT STROKE.
IT LOOKS LIKE THE SAND PEOPLE DID THIS, ALL RIGHT.
LOOK, THERE'S GAFFI STICKS, BANTHA TRACKS...
THEY DIDN'T.
BUT WE ARE MEANT TO THINK THEY DID.

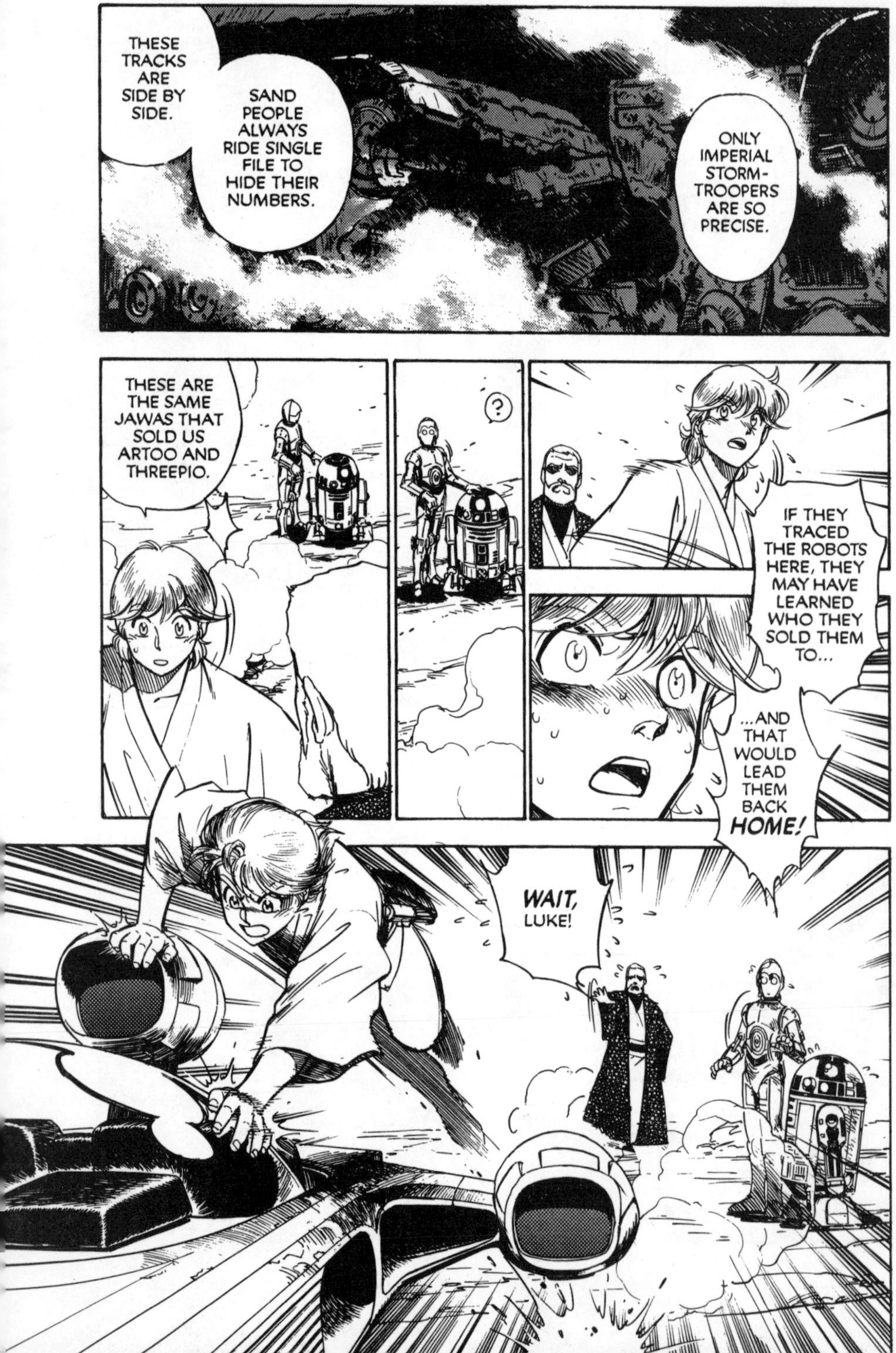
THESE TRACKS ARE SIDE BY SIDE.
SAND PEOPLE ALWAYS RIDE SINGLE FILE TO HIDE THEIR NUMBERS.
ONLY IMPERIAL STORM-TROOPERS ARE SO PRECISE.
THESE ARE THE SAME JAWAS THAT SOLD US ARTOO AND THREEPIO.
?
IF THEY TRACED THE ROBOTS HERE, THEY MAY HAVE LEARNED WHO THEY SOLD THEM TO...
...AND THAT WOULD LEAD THEM BACK *HOME!*
WAIT, LUKE!

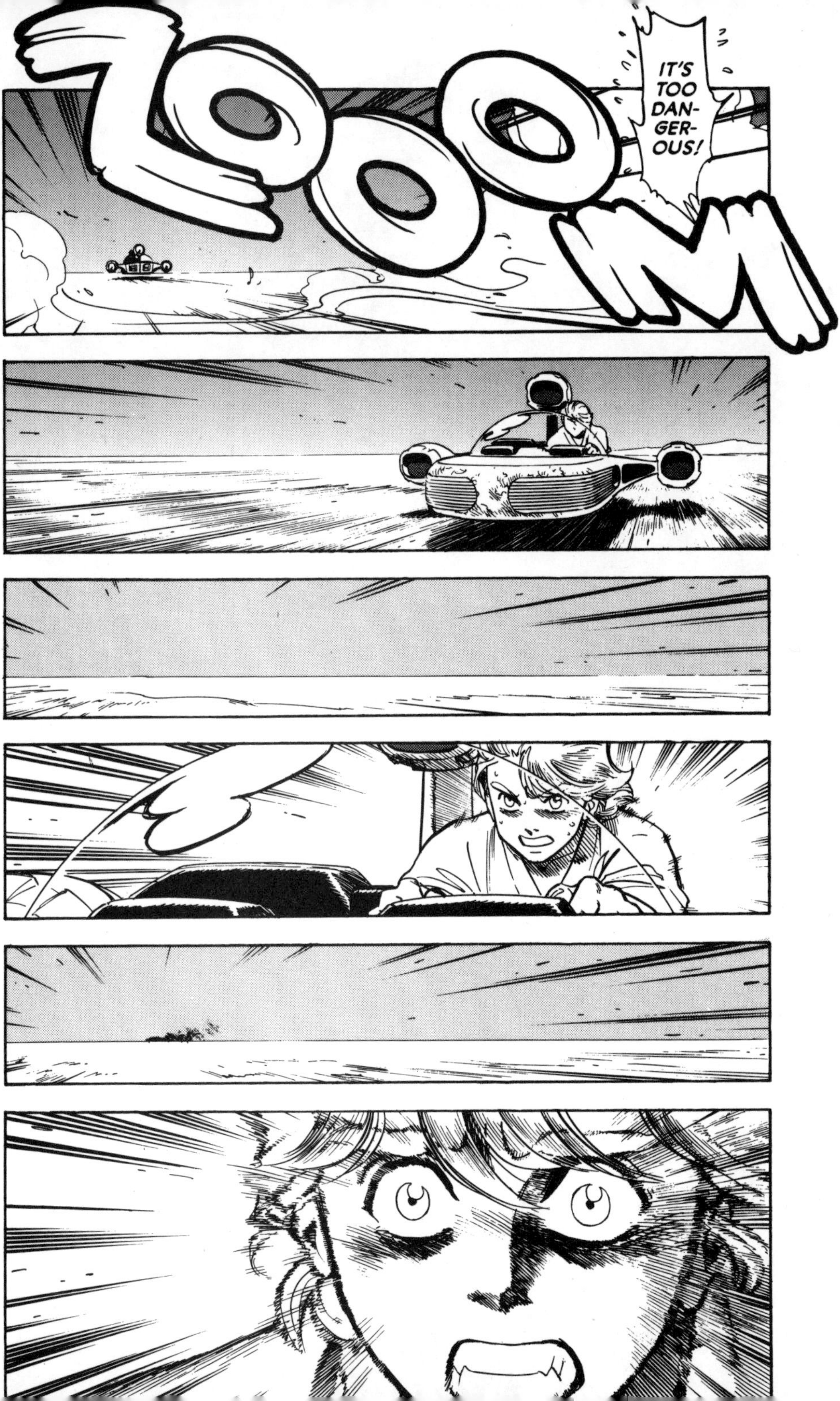
ZOOOM
IT'S TOO DAN-GER-OUS!

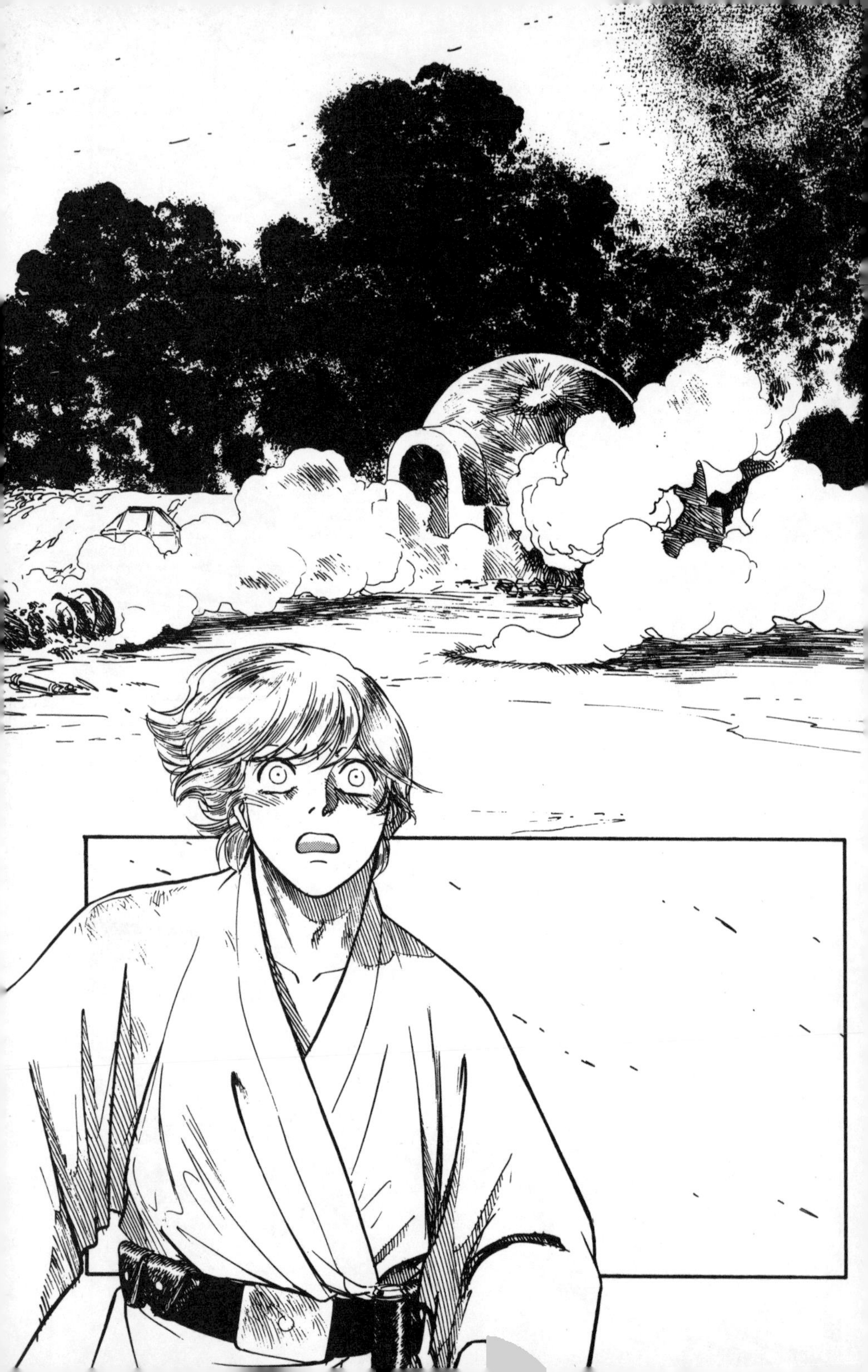

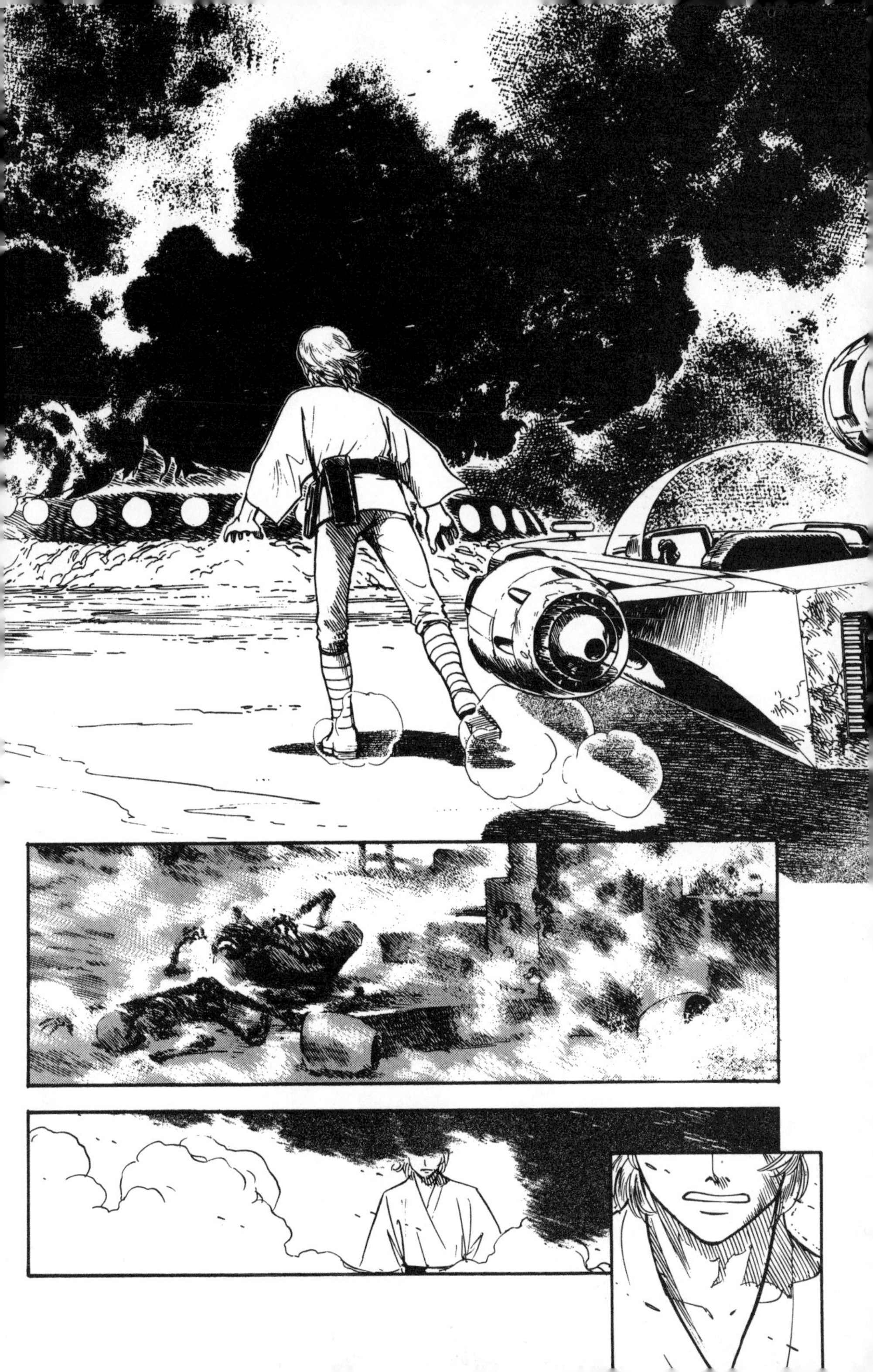

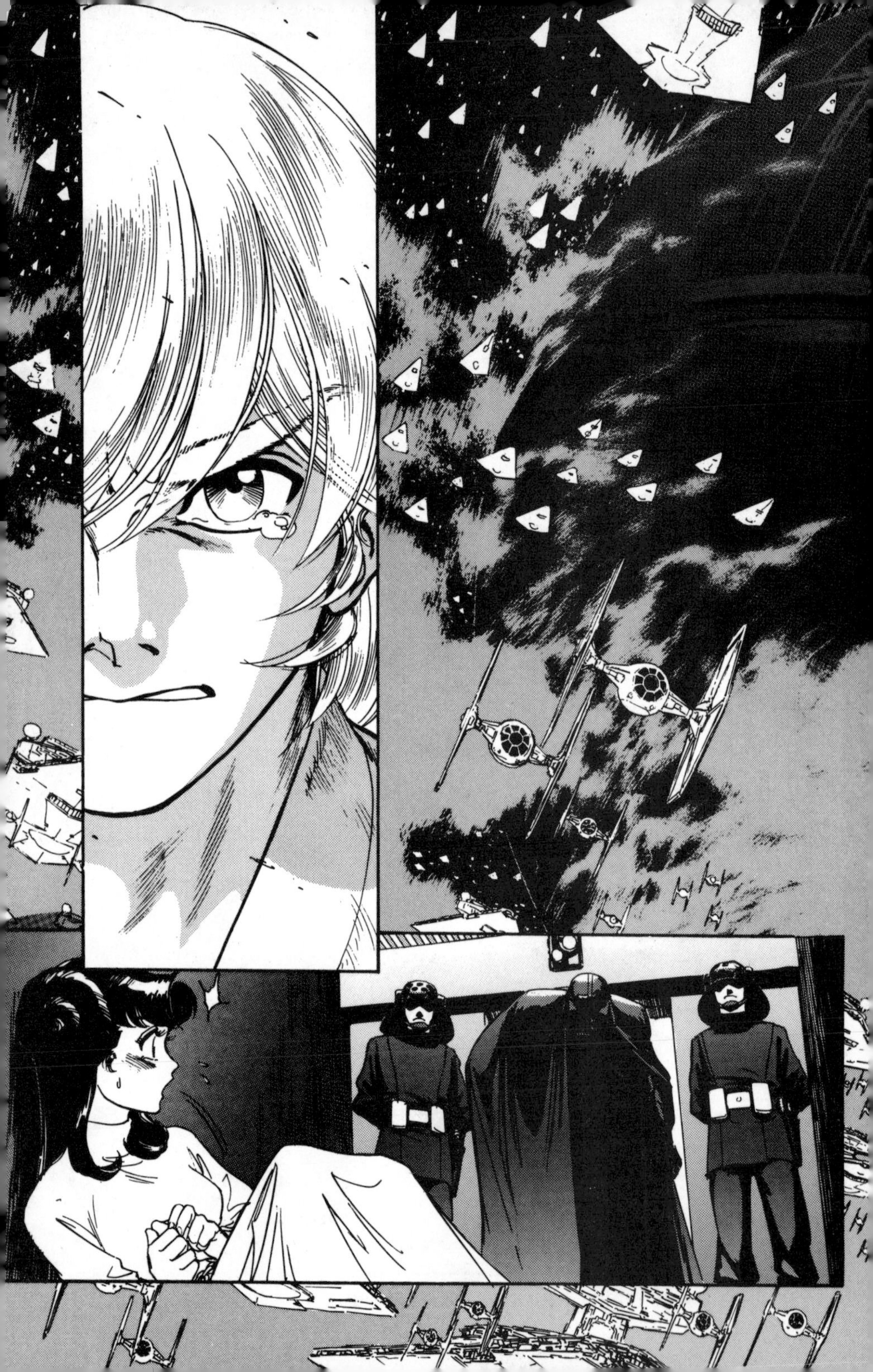

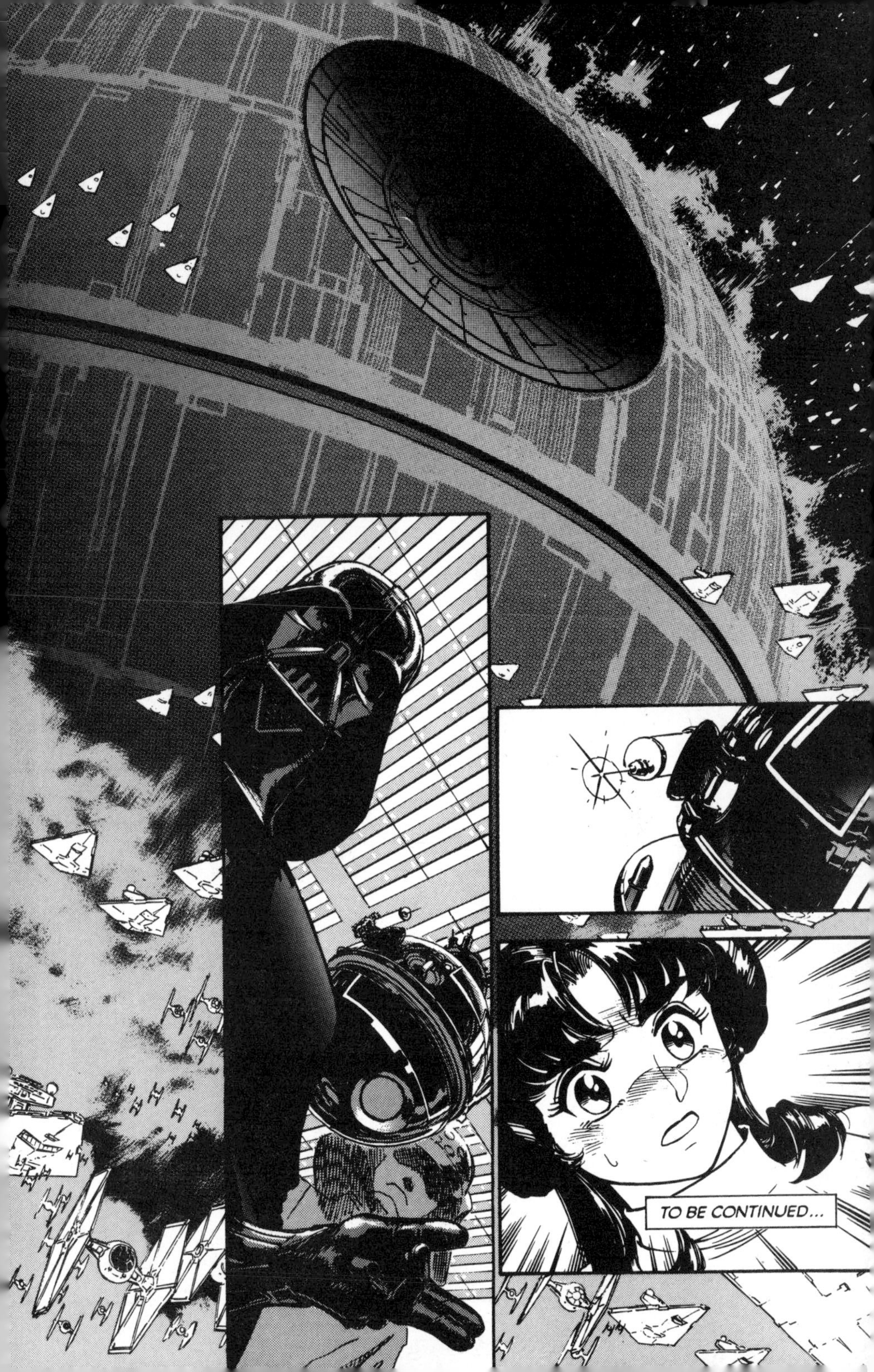
TO BE CONTINUED...

スター・ウォーズ HISAO TAMAKI SKETCH GALLERY

The following are sketches by artist Hisao Tamaki, done in preparation for his work on STAR WARS: A NEW HOPE — MANGA.

DARTH VADER

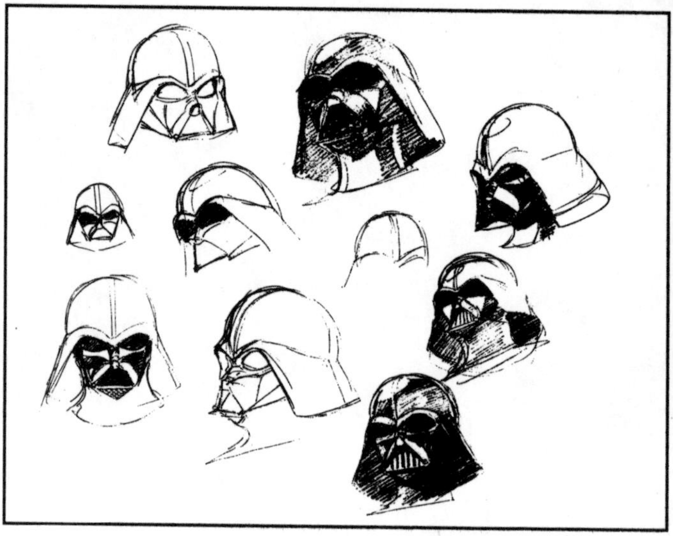

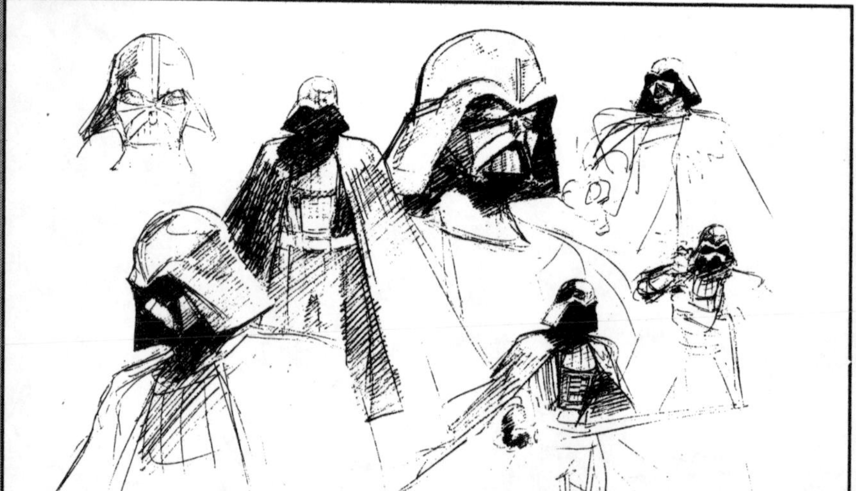

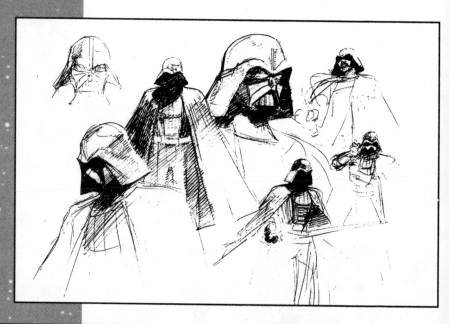

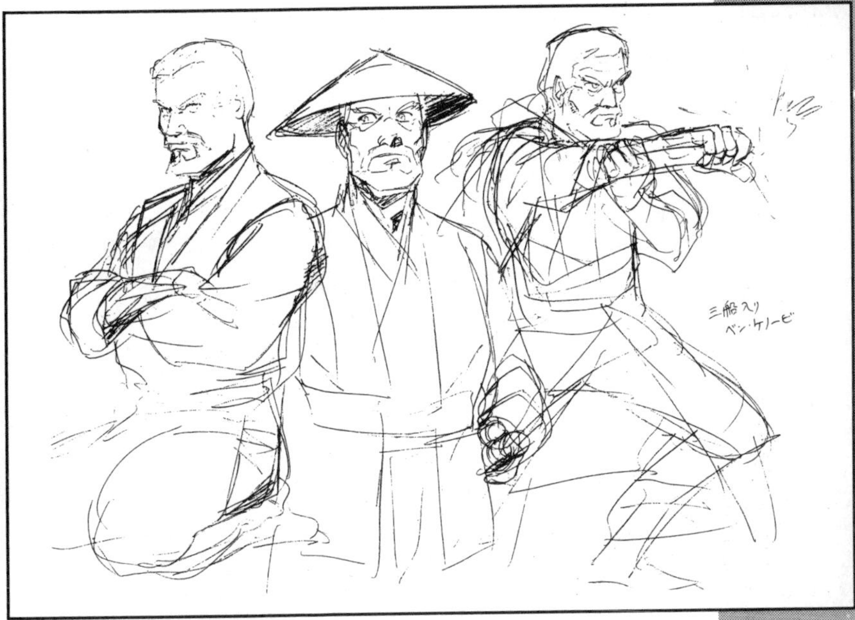
三船入り
ベン・ケノービ

▲ OBI-WAN KENOBI
▶ LUKE SKYWALKER
▼ C-3PO AND R2-D2

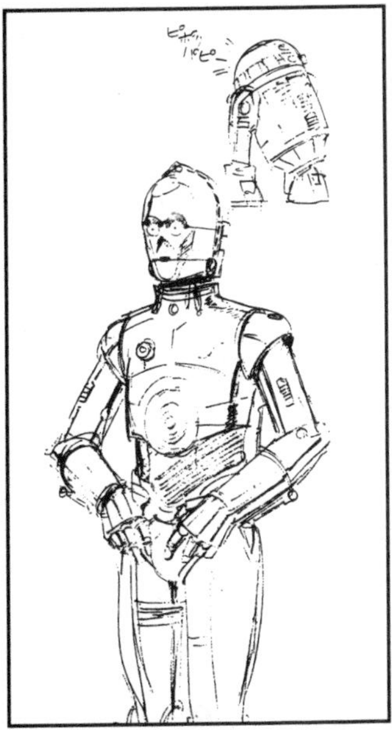

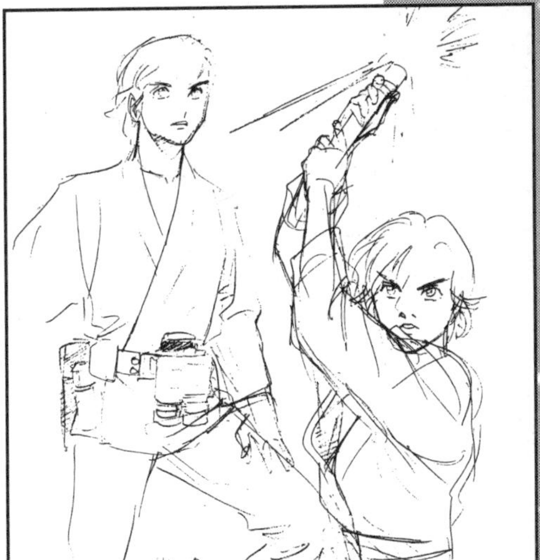
ルーク

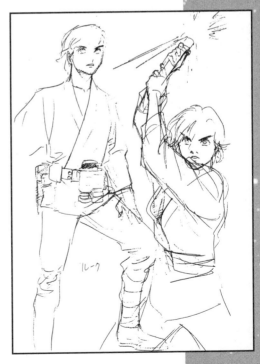

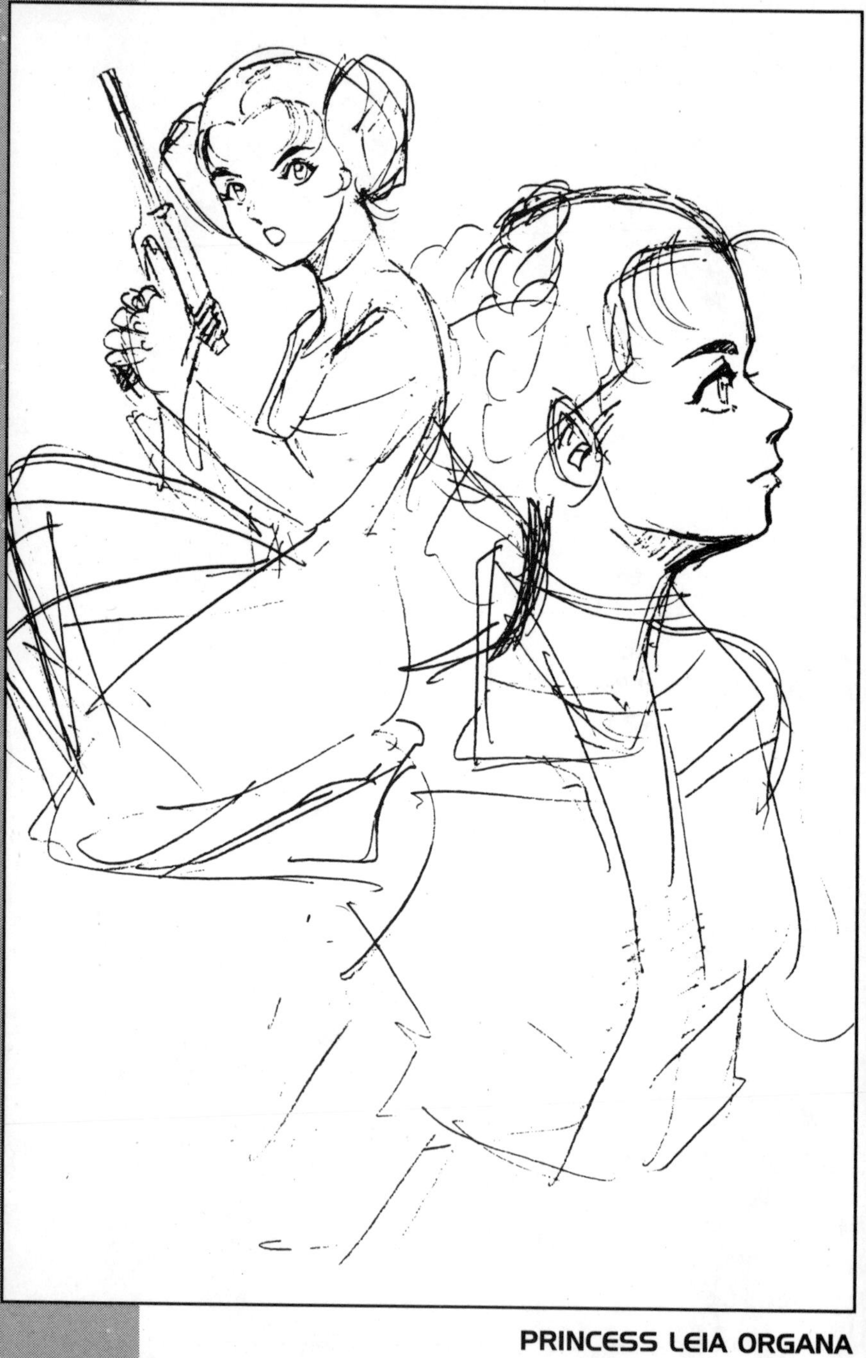

PRINCESS LEIA ORGANA

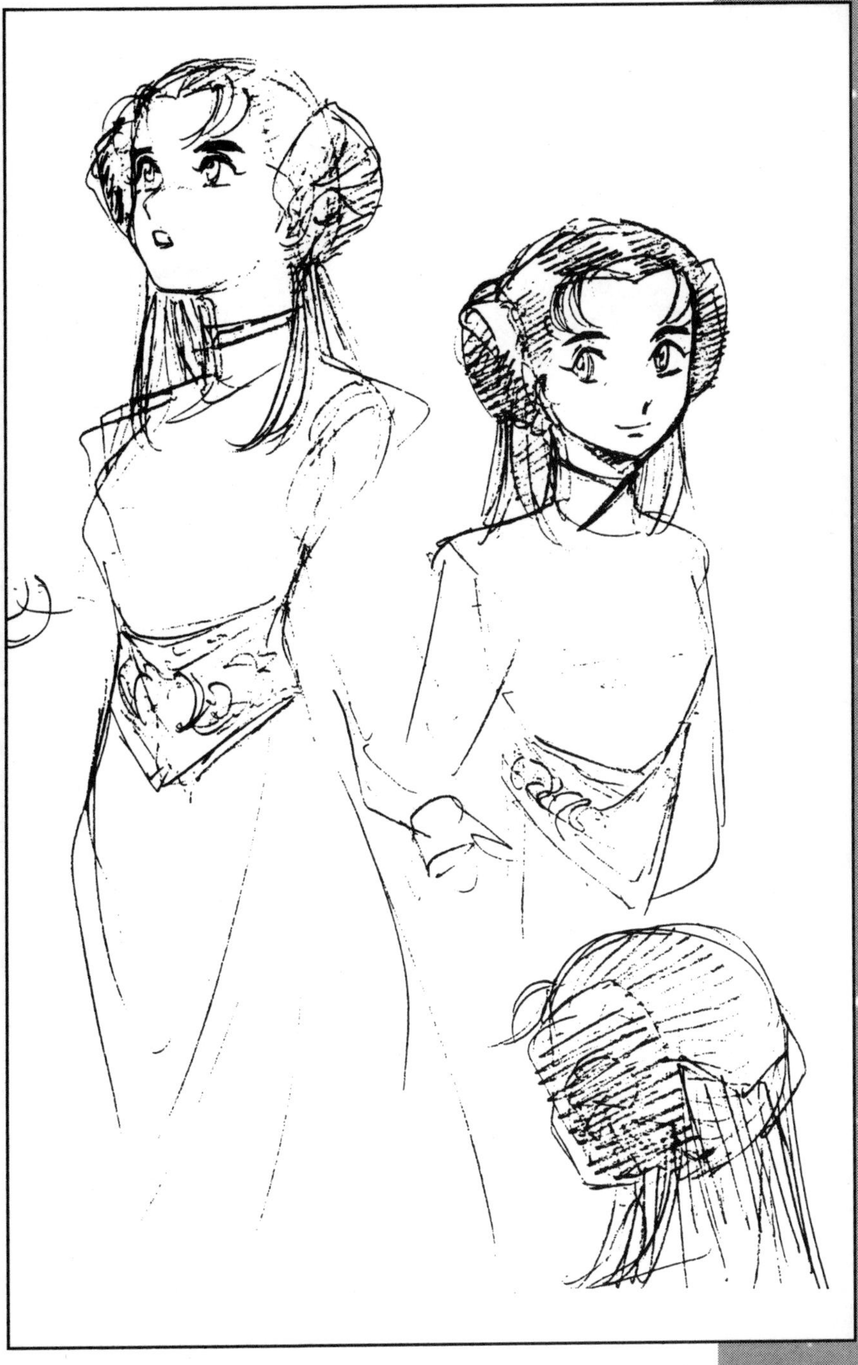

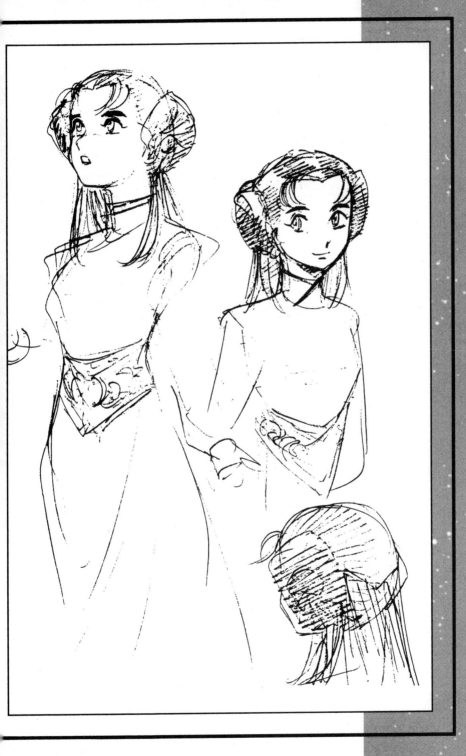

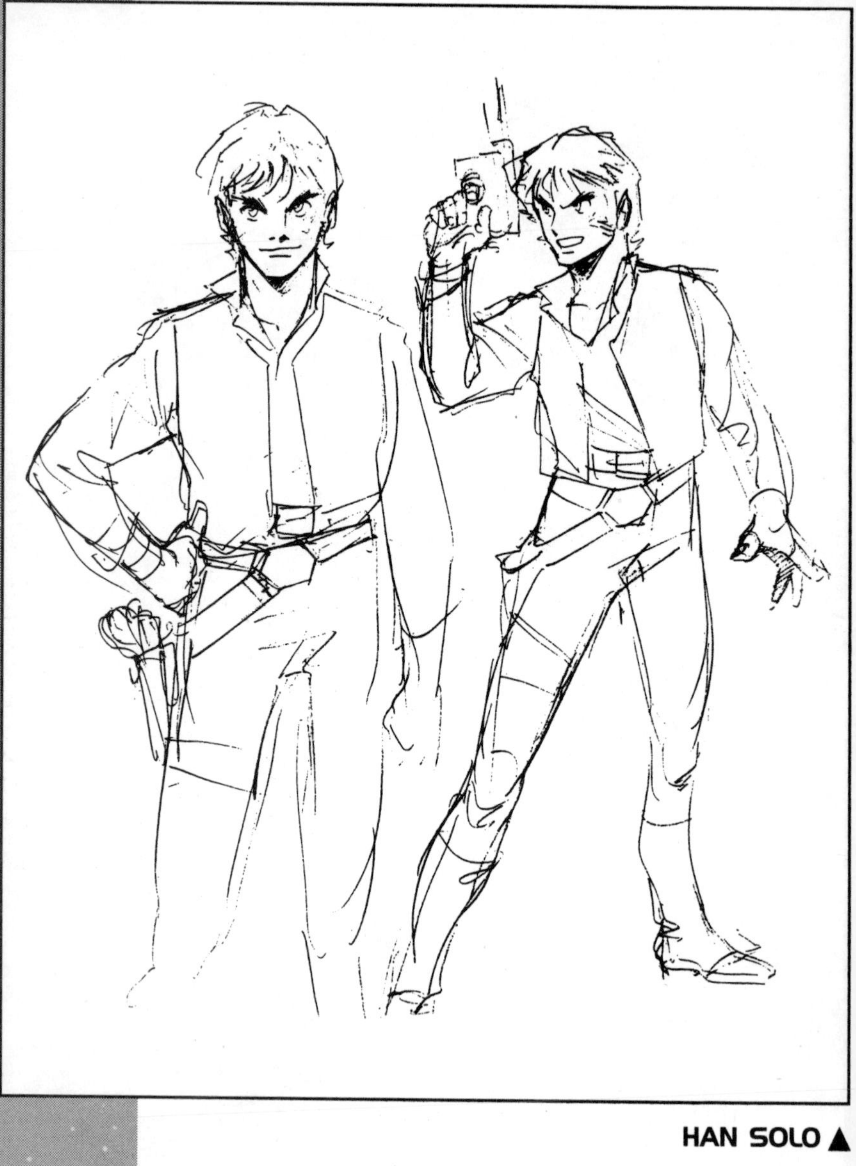

HAN SOLO ▲

HAN SOLO AND CHEWBACCA ▶

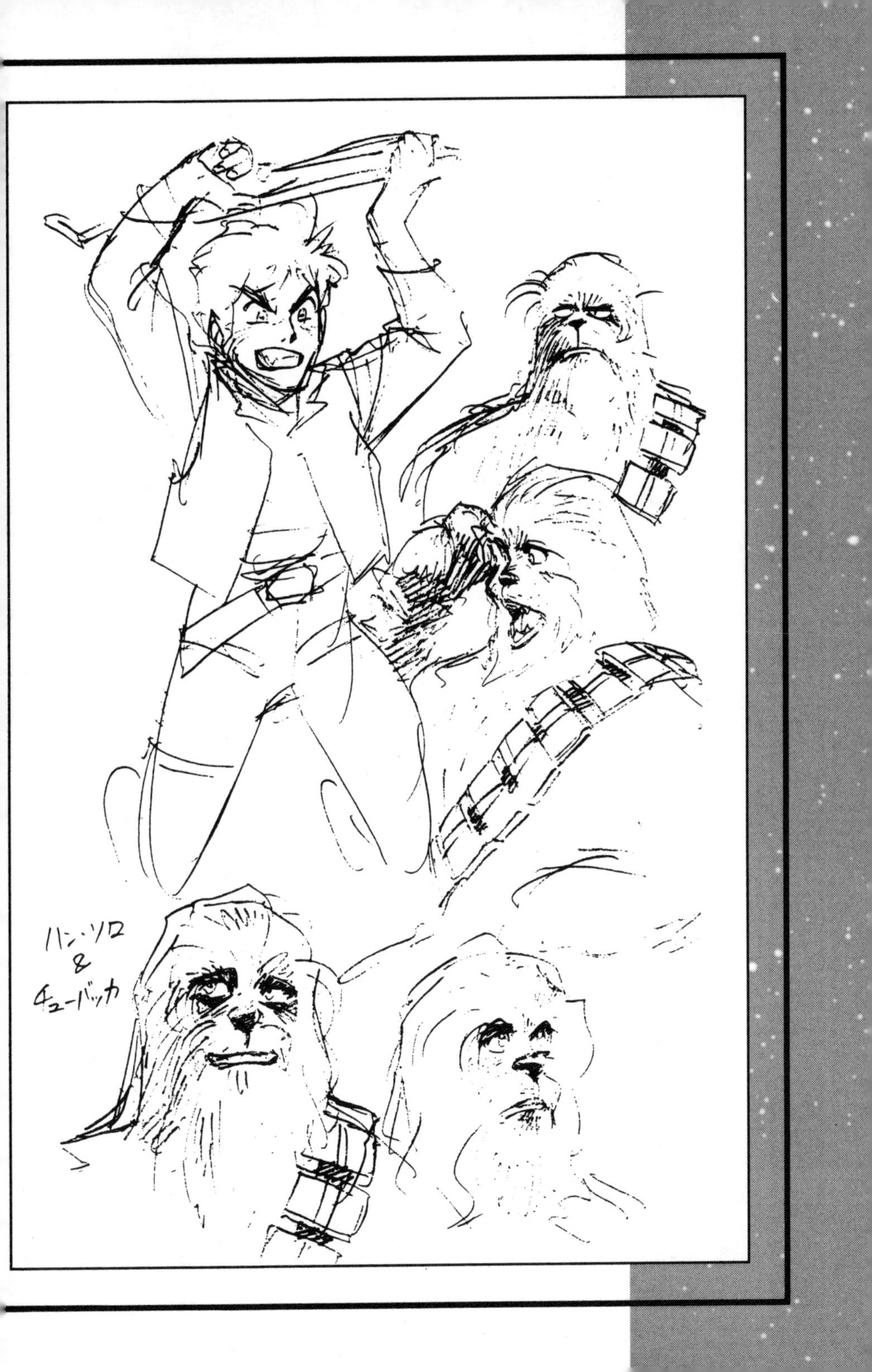
ハン・ソロ
&
チューバッカ

HAN SOLO
PRINCESS LEIA ORGANA
LUKE SKYWALKER

The following are sketches by cover artist Adam Warren, done in preparation for the final cover of STAR WARS: A NEW HOPE — MANGA volume one.

スター・ウォーズ
ADAM WARREN
SKETCH GALLERY

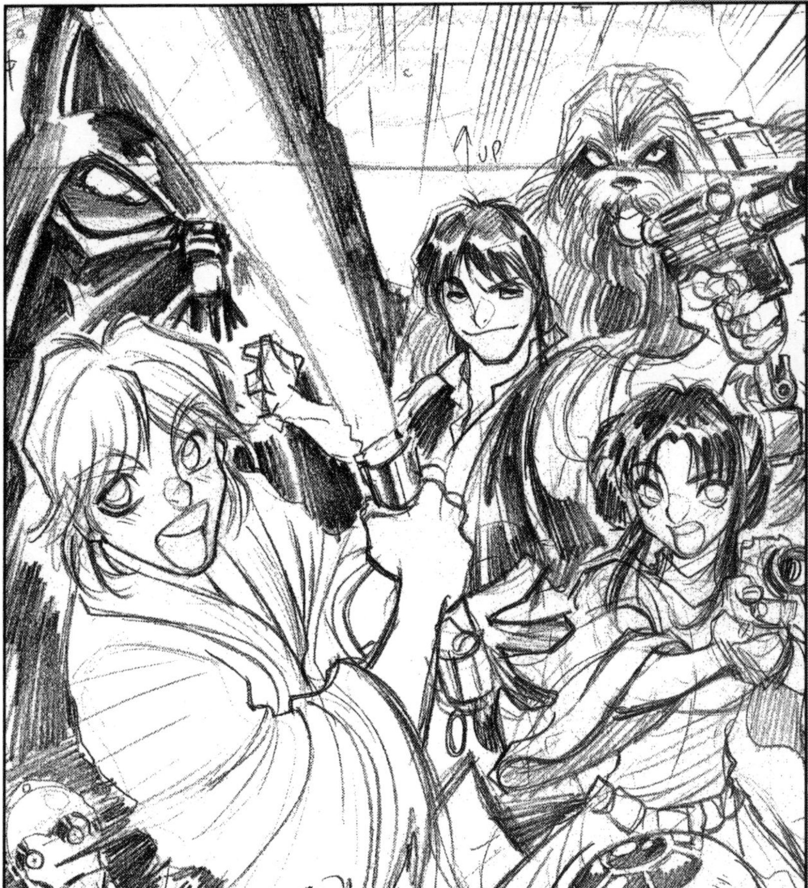
UP

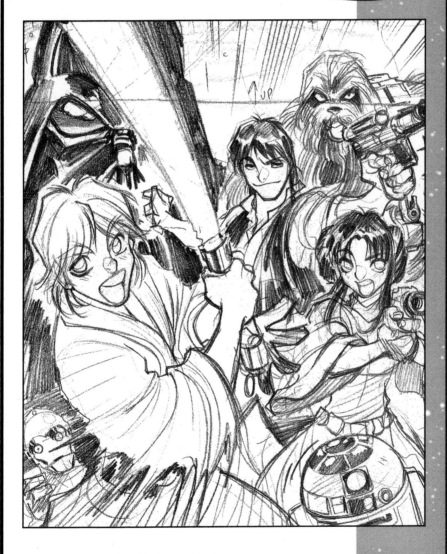

ALTERNATE COVER SKETCH FOR STAR WARS MANGA VOLUME ONE

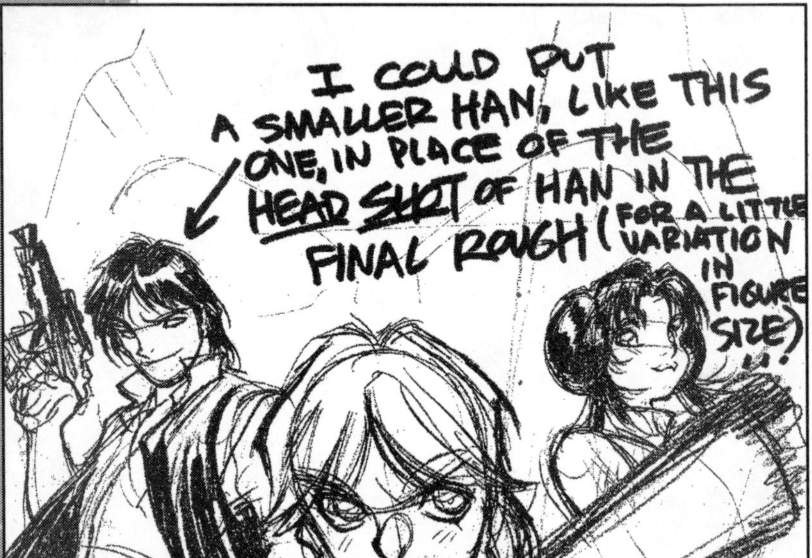
I COULD PUT A SMALLER HAN, LIKE THIS ONE, IN PLACE OF THE HEAD SHOT OF HAN IN THE FINAL ROUGH (FOR A LITTLE VARIATION IN FIGURE SIZE) ...!

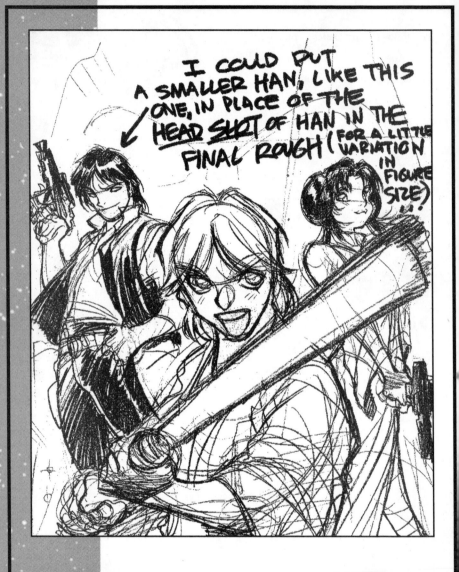

ALTERNATE COVER SKETCH FOR
STAR WARS MANGA VOLUME ONE

ADAPTED FROM AN ORIGINAL SCRIPT BY GEORGE LUCAS

ILLUSTRATION BY HISAO TAMAKI

スター・ウォーズ 1

新たなる希望〈上〉

LETTERING AND ART RETOUCH BY TOM ORZECHOWSKI

COVER ART BY ADAM WARREN

COVER COLORS BY JOSEPH WIGHT

SPECIAL THANKS TO ALLAN KAUSCH AND LUCY AUTREY WILSON AT LUCAS LICENSING

SPECIAL THANKS TO MONTY SHELDON, EVELYN WOOD, AND AMADOR CISNEROS

BOOK DESIGN BY CARY GRAZZINI

EDITED BY DAVID LAND

PUBLISHED BY MIKE RICHARDSON

Published by Dark Horse Comics, Inc., 10956 SE Main Street, Milwaukie, OR 97222

ISBN: 1-56971-362-6 First edition: July 1998

10 9 8 7 6 5 4

PRINTED IN THE UNITED STATES OF AMERICA

スター・ウォーズ BACKLIST
DARK HORSE'S COMPLETE LINE OF スター・ウォーズ SPECIALTY BOOKS

IN DEADLY PURSUIT
ISBN: 1-56971-109-7 $16.95

THE REBEL STORM
ISBN: 1-56971-106-2 $16.95

ESCAPE TO HOTH
ISBN: 1-56971-093-7 $16.95

THE EARLY ADVENTURES
ISBN: 1-56971-178-X $19.95

HAN SOLO AT STARS' END
ISBN: 1-56971-254-9 $6.95

A NEW HOPE
ISBN: 1-56971-213-1 $9.95

THE EMPIRE STRIKES BACK
ISBN: 1-56971-234-4 $9.95

RETURN OF THE JEDI
ISBN: 1-56971-235-2 $9.95

DARK EMPIRE
ISBN: 1-56971-073-2 $17.95

DARK EMPIRE II
ISBN: 1-56971-119-4 $17.95

EMPIRE'S END
ISBN: 1-56971-306-5 $5.95

DEATH, LIES, & TREACHERY
ISBN: 1-56971-311-1 $12.95

SOLDIER FOR THE EMPIRE
ISBN: 1-56971-155-0 $24.95

REBEL AGENT
ISBN: 1-56971-156-9 $24.95

JEDI KNIGHT
1-56971-157-7 $24.95

SOLDIER FOR THE EMPIRE SC
1-56971-348-0 $14.95

漫画 BACKLIST

DARK HORSE'S COMPLETE LINE OF 漫画 SPECIALTY BOOKS

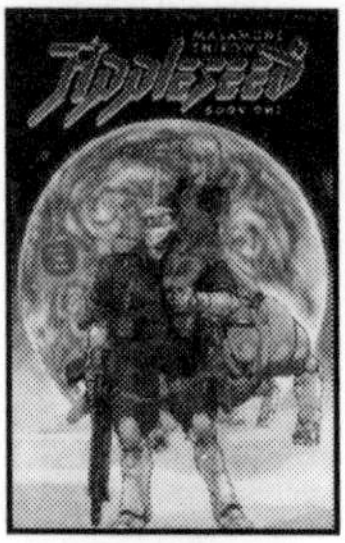

BOOK ONE
ISBN: 1-56971-070-8 $14.95

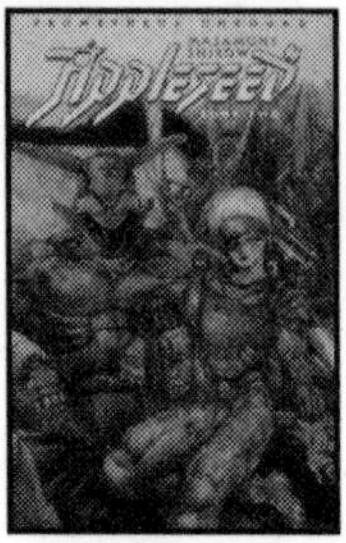

BOOK TWO
ISBN: 1-56971-071-6 $14.95

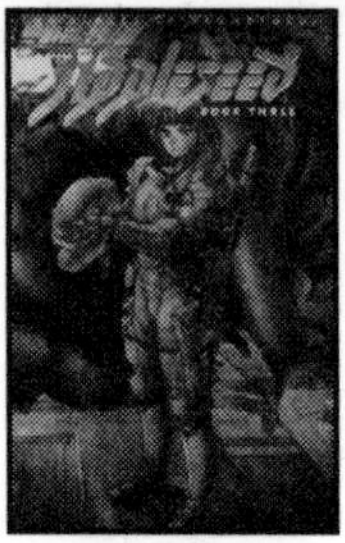

BOOK THREE
ISBN: 1-56971-072-4 $14.95

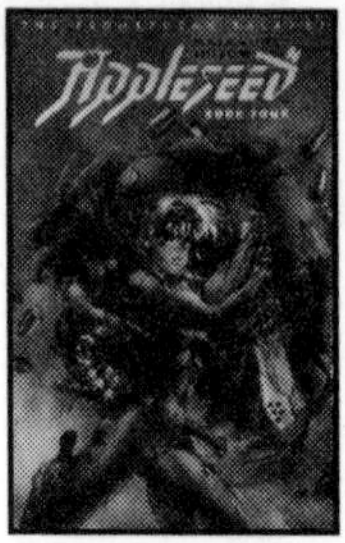

BOOK FOUR
ISBN: 1-56971-074-0 $14.95

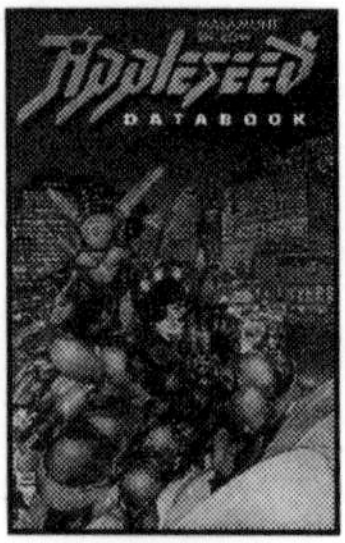
DATABOOK

DATABOOK
ISBN: 1-56971-103-8 $12.95

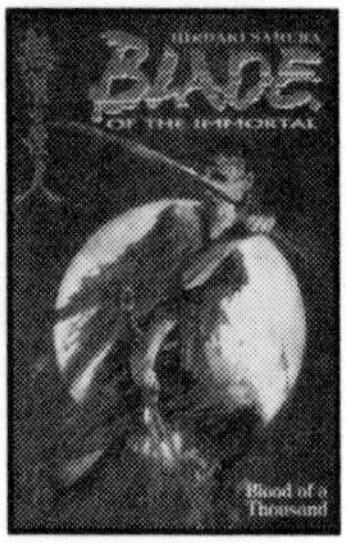
BLADE
OF THE IMMORTAL
Blood of a Thousand

BLOOD OF A THOUSAND
ISBN: 1-56971-239-5 $12.95

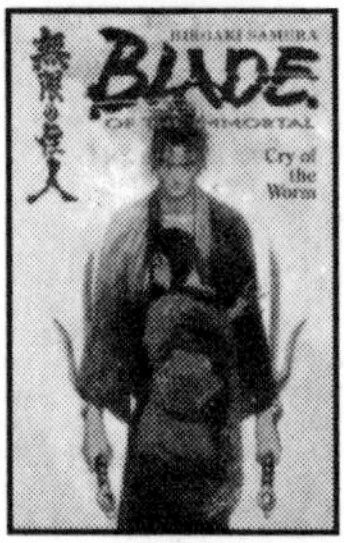
BLADE
Cry of the Worm

CRY OF THE WORM
ISBN: 1-56971-300-6 $12.95

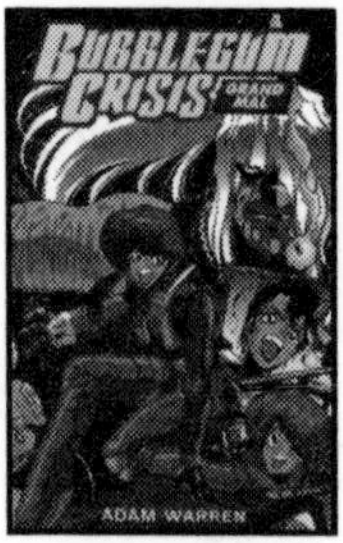
BUBBLEGUM CRISIS
GRAND MAL
ADAM WARREN

GRAND MAL
ISBN: 1-56971-120-8 $14.95

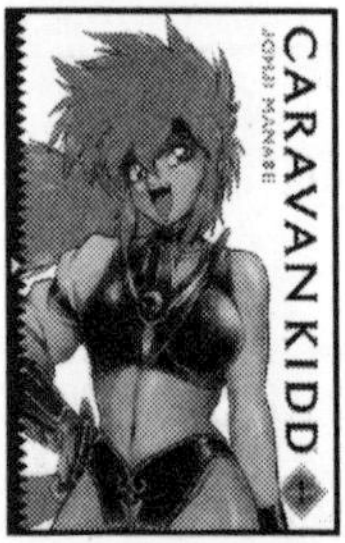
CARAVAN KIDD
JOHJI MANABE

VOLUME ONE
ISBN: 1-56971-260-3 $19.95

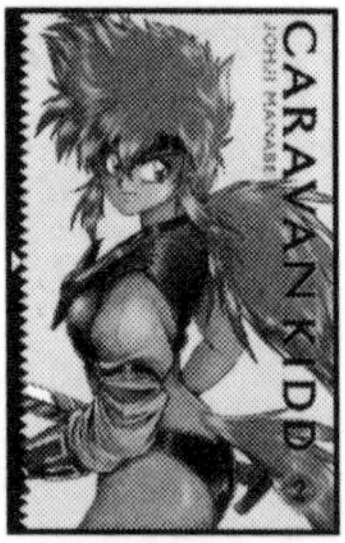
CARAVAN KIDD

VOLUME TWO
ISBN: 1-56971-324-3 $19.95

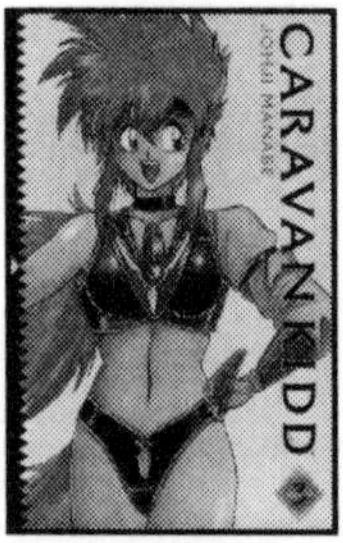
CARAVAN KIDD
JOHJI MANABE

VOLUME THREE
ISBN: 1-5-6971-338-3 $19.95

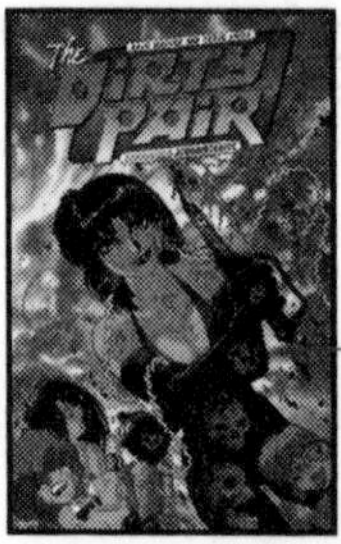
DIRTY PAIR

DANGEROUS ACQUAINTANCES
ISBN: 1-56971-227-1 $12.95

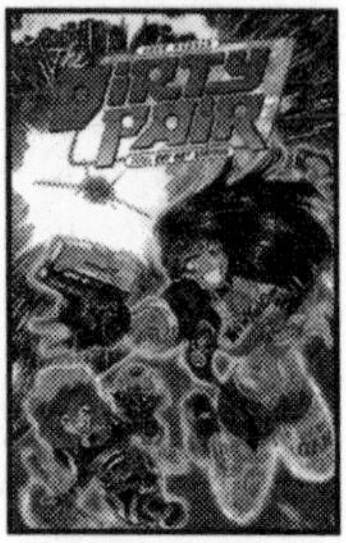
DIRTY PAIR

FATAL BUT NOT SERIOUS
ISBN: 1-56971-172-0 $14.95

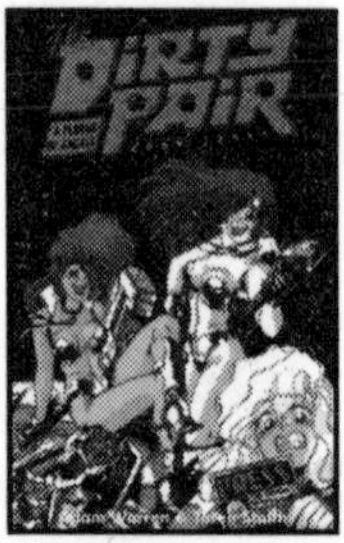
DIRTY PAIR

A PLAGUE OF ANGELS
ISBN: 1-56971-029-5 $12.95

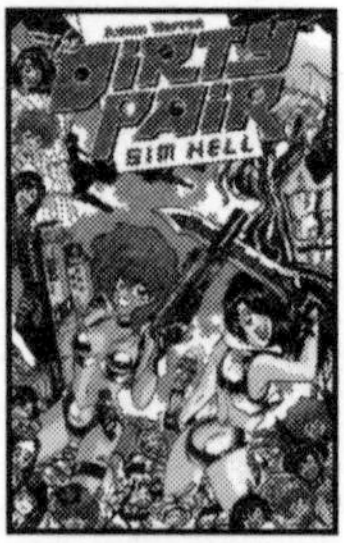
DIRTY PAIR
SIM HELL

SIM HELL
ISBN: 1-56971-159-3 $13.95

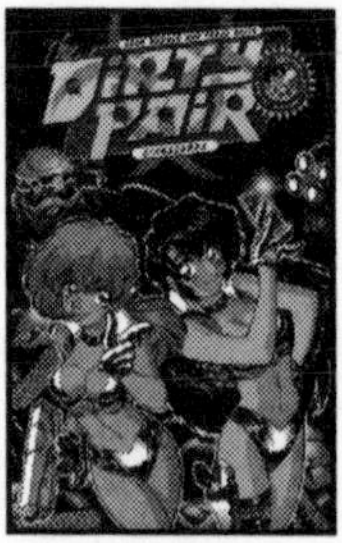
DIRTY PAIR

BIOHAZARDS
ISBN:1-56917-339-1 $12.95

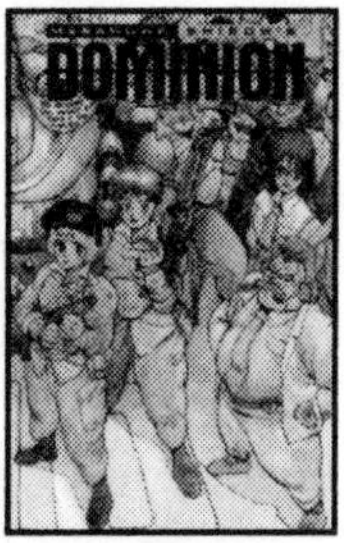
DOMINION

DOMINION
ISBN: 1-56971-160-7 $14.95

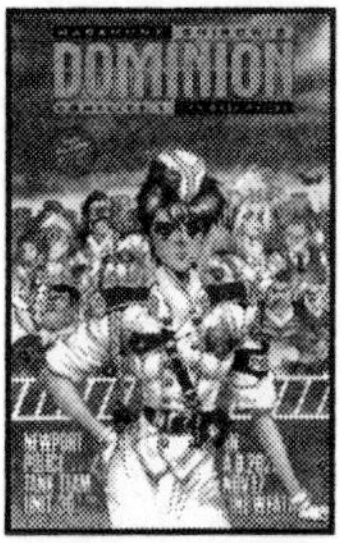
DOMINION

CONFLICT 1: NO MORE NOISE
ISBN: 1-56971-233-6 $14.95

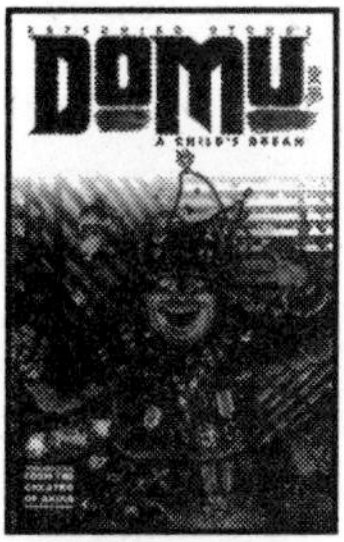
DOMU
A CHILD'S DREAM

A CHILD'S DREAM
ISBN: 1-56971-140-2 $17.95

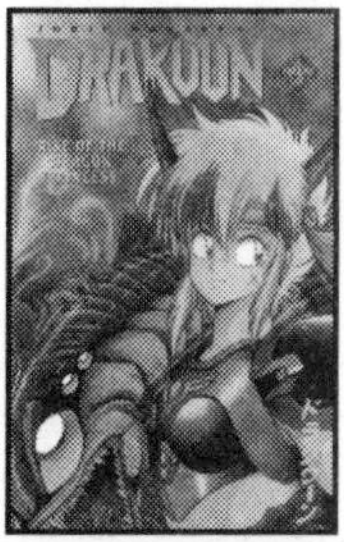

RISE OF THE DRAGON PRINCESS
ISBN: 1-56971-302-2 $12.95

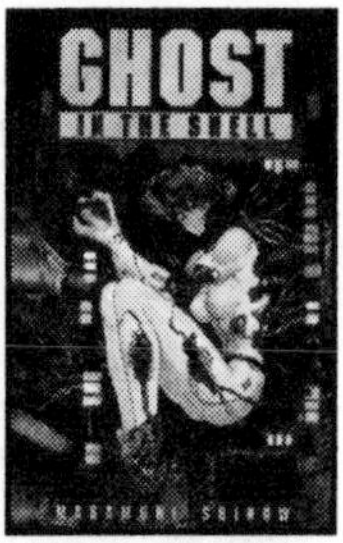
GHOST

GHOST IN THE SHELL
ISBN: 1-56971-081-3 $24.95

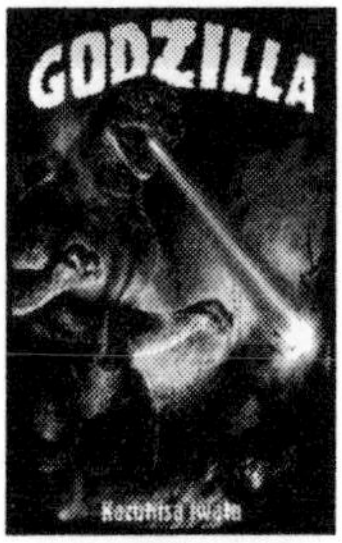
GODZILLA

GODZILLA
ISBN: 1-56971-063-5 $17.95

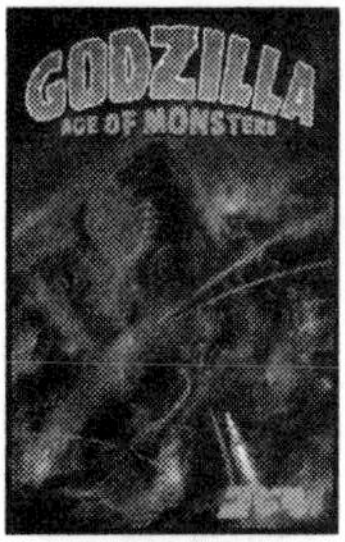
GODZILLA
AGE OF MONSTERS

AGE OF MONSTERS
ISBN: 1-56971-277-8 $17.95

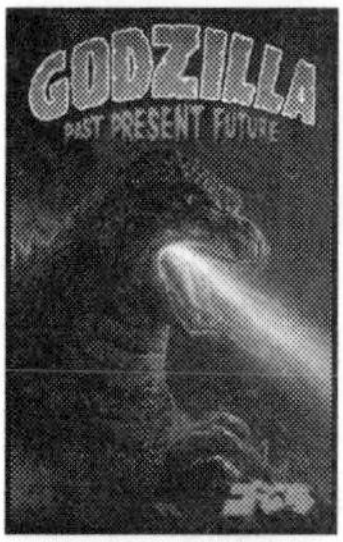
GODZILLA
PAST PRESENT FUTURE

PAST, PRESENT, AND FUTURE
ISBN: 1-56971-278-6 $17.95

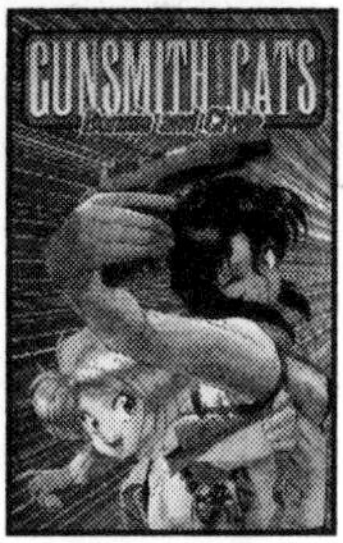
GUNSMITH CATS

BONNIE & CLYDE
ISBN: 1-56971-215-8 $12.95

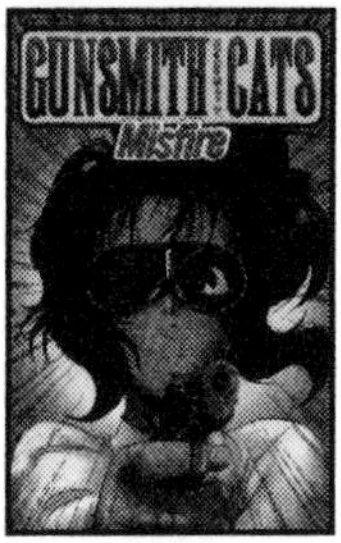
GUNSMITH CATS
Misfire

MISFIRE
ISBN: 1-56971-253-0 $12.95

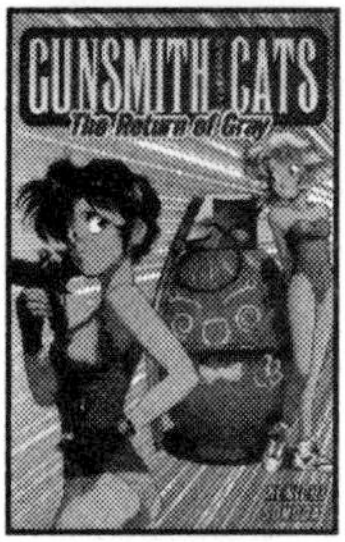
GUNSMITH CATS
The Return of Gray

RETURN OF GRAY
ISBN: 1-56971-299-9 $17.95

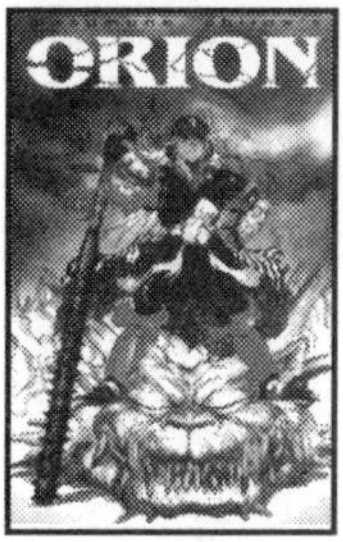
ORION

ORION
ISBN: 1-56971-148-8 $17.95

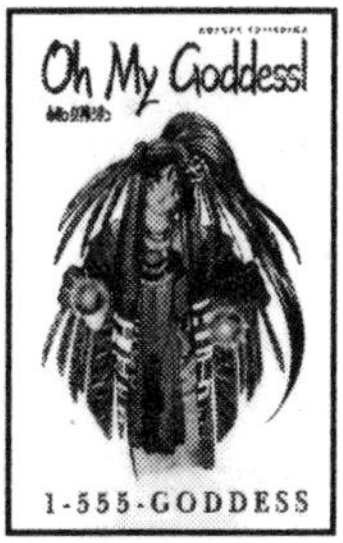
Oh My Goddess!
1-555-GODDESS

1-555-GODDESS
ISBN: 1-56971-207-7 $12.95

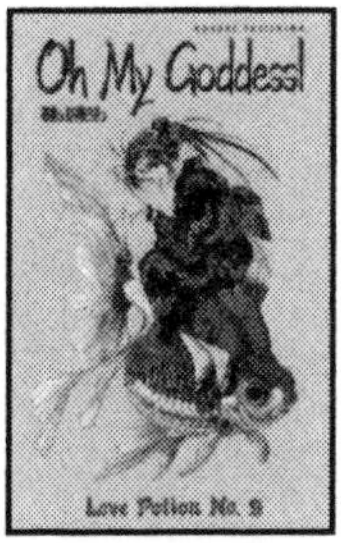
Oh My Goddess!
Love Potion No. 9

LOVE POTION NO. 9
ISBN: 1-56971-252-2 $12.95

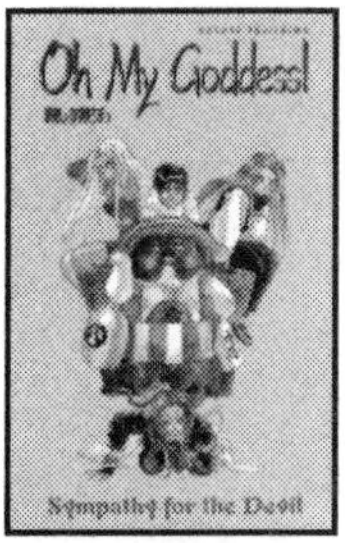
Oh My Goddess!
Sympathy for the Devil

SYMPATHY FOR THE DEVIL
ISBN: 1-56971-329-4 $12.95

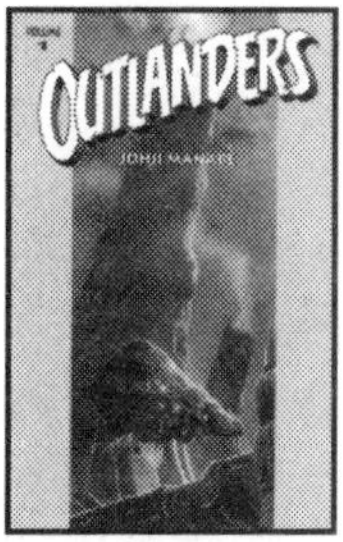
OUTLANDERS

VOLUME 1
ISBN: 1-56971-161-5 $13.95